Turn Right

A JOURNEY TO PURPOSEFUL CAREERS

Inez Natalia

ISBN 978-6-0268-5034-8

How do you trust a child to take a roller-coaster ride?

Ask my parents.

Table of Contents

Let's go on a journey together !

You are invited to be not only a reader
but also the writer, creator and designer
of your own story and journey.

A Note to You

There are many reasons why people want to start reading a book. Yet the book, itself, always has its own hopes and wishes for its readers. This book, in particular, has been created for you. It was written with you in mind. You are the reason you are reading this book.

Are you looking for answers? Do you want a career that gives you fulfillment and endless development? Do you want to be in a state of contentment, every single day? Then, my friends, this book is for you. It is here to give you the courage to ask questions and, more importantly, to give you the courage to finally discover the answers.

Primarily, you need to know what this book is not about.

It is not another book written by an individual who wants to influence you into becoming something you are not. It is also not motivational mumbo-jumbo telling you to 'follow your passion no matter what'. What you will find here are provocative thoughts, offered not only through statements and sentences, but in the form of sparks in your head and butterflies in your stomach.

This book invites you not only to be a reader but also to be the writer, creator, and designer of your own story and journey. It was created to be your best friend: something to assist you on your journey in discovering the reason why YOU should be here, on earth.

It is also not the intention of this book to make you choose between being a good person with no money or being a heartless person with a lot of money. Throughout our journey together, you will come to understand that, with the right design and approach, pursuing a career is not the same as just paying your bills. Instead, a career is a vehicle for realizing the reasons for your existence while at the same time helping you reach your own personal goals: ones that are essential to your life.

Now, you need to know what this book is about.

This book is about you. It is also about me. As you continue to read, you will find stories from my own journey, as well as stories from the journeys of others. It will highlight some of our turning points within the reality of the career scene, not to mention in life itself. I want these stories to help you, to provide clarity as you take your first steps in your own exciting journey.

I have a selfish reason for writing this book: a selfish reason that drives a selfless act. That reason is 'Purpose' that I owe to the universe and to myself. Purpose is the sole reason I could not shift to an extreme direction, even when many adventures and opportunities—or should I say temptations—appeared before me. It is not raw ambition for achievement or recognition that drives me, nor am I checking a to-do list of my life's agenda. Purpose gives meaning to my existence.

This book is a concrete form of action I took in consciously realizing my Purpose. I hope throughout this journey that you will find the drive to start your own. I hope it will help you discover the life that not only gives you a sense of living, but ultimately the feeling of being ALIVE. I hope you will find the courage to start living purposefully.

Part 1

"Knock, knock."

"Who's there?"

"Sometimes it is the people no one imagines anything of

who do the things that no one can imagine."

Christopher Morcom (The Imitation Game, 2014)

Chapter 1

And It Begins...

While growing up, I was always anxious about my future. As a kid, it was easy to define success—well, at least in my society it was. Mainly, success was judged by the praise you got when you became the top student, when you succeeded in making something for the first time, or when you won a school competition. As I got older, I began to understand that people constantly need to make decisions in life. But, every decision has its consequences. These consequences lead to the next intersection where we need to make yet another decision, which has further consequences. I began to realize that, because of this, success, itself, was not so easy to define.

I remember one morning perfectly, because it was the fateful occasion that marked the first turning point in my life.

It was August 17, 2006, and I was in my final year of high school, a year during which I was mostly confused. I didn't know what university I wanted to go to, let alone what subject I was to major in. Yet, it wasn't merely because I had no idea what I wanted for I had always known I would like to get a scholarship to study abroad. And, I had also wished to be rich and have a comfortable, happy life with my family.

No, the main reason for this confusion was I hated living in my country. I hated the education system and the corruption in the government. I even hated the traffic.

I didn't feel connected with the culture, and I also felt bored. I thought there wasn't any hope for my nation to become any better. At that time, my teenage self told me there were much better societies and cultures outside of my own. My major disconnection from my roots, and my despair over my surroundings, were the main triggers that prompted me to start creating an 'escape plan'.

My escape plan was pretty simple: I just needed to figure out what major to take that would lead to a high-paying career abroad. That was my state of mind during my final year of high school. It was all about what I wanted my future to look like. But, on August 17, 2006, my life changed forever.

That morning I came to school early for our annual flag-raising ceremony in celebration of Indonesia's 61st Independence Day. I thought it would be just another ceremony, one I had always attended since primary school. I would be bored to death and was ready to incessantly complain about the intolerable heat. But, what eventually happened was something I had never expected in all my years of attending it.

During one section, a student representative had to give a speech, and the honor went to a friend of mine. Her name was Debby. She began her speech with a story and an invitation.

Debby invited us all to take some time to look back into the past. She took us on a journey, telling us about the heroes who had fought and sacrificed their lives for Indonesia's independence. These brave heroes who were as young as we were, had given their lives, their blood, their sweat and their tears for our country, and for the generations that came after them.

Then, Debby paused for a few moments, and asked us to imagine something: What if these heroes were alive in our times? What would they feel and what would they think, seeing the young people of our generation, people who were deeply skeptical about the state of the nation? Imagine how hurt they would feel to learn that the generation they gave their lives for would rather move abroad in search of comfort and luxury. If all the great talents of Indonesia preferred to leave their homeland, who would be left to make Indonesia better?

It was a slap in my face. It felt like my friend had taken the stage in order to speak to me directly. It was a wake-up call from my seventeen-year long slumber. I hadn't expected it. I had always thought I wanted a comfortable life without any concern for money. I was always complaining about everything bad that was happening to me and around me.

Before that fateful day, it had never crossed my mind I was actually part of the problem plaguing my nation. All I did was rant, adding hatred and negativity to my surroundings, subconsciously engaging others to think badly about their country as well. I kept complaining without thinking of any particular solution to make my country better.

From that day forward, I made up my mind to take a fixed, sharp turn. No matter how the journey might turn out, I decided I wanted to be part of the solution. I wanted to be part of a group of people who would contribute and strive for the improvement of the nation, and even the world.

I knew there wouldn't be a finishing line, a peak achievement where I could say "Finished" before taking a bow to a round of applause. It would be a long, endless, difficult journey; but, it would be fulfilling.

So, *this* became my new definition of success: to contribute to, and become part of, the solution for Indonesia.

It's Never Too Early

After experiencing that profound personal moment, I tried to formulate a plan so I could play a more significant role in making Indonesia a better nation. I thought I would need to work in public service or hold some sort of position that would enable me to play a role in the global arena, representing my country.

Therefore, I chose to major in International Relations. I expected I would have enough power to make a significant change in the country by the time I was forty or fifty. At that time, I thought in order for me to make a significant change in society, I needed to have position, money, and countless followers. I thought I might not achieve that stage in anything less than 30 years.

Thinking I still had a lot of time, I spent the first three years of my university life gaining knowledge while immersing myself in different kinds of event-organizing experiences on campus. To my mind, university life shouldn't have been complicated. It should have been a simple time where we had the freedom to explore and have fun. I didn't know then there was something bigger than anything I had ever imagined waiting for me outside those lecture halls. Looking back now, I realize that International Relations was probably not the right major for me. But, it doesn't matter, because that decision led me to something unexpectedly significant.

In my third year of university, during an on-campus event, there was open recruitment for a global organization. By sheer coincidence, I joined an organization called AIESEC.

I found out later that its mission was to develop leadership potential in young people. It was independent and youth-led. I was exposed to a new world where thousands of young people all across the earth actually had the ambition to make a real difference.

During my five years with AIESEC I had the opportunity to explore seventeen different countries scattered across three different continents. I lived in Cambodia for a year, where I had the opportunity to lead the national operation as president of the organization along with a team of nine people from six different nations.

AIESEC envisions peace and fulfillment of humankind's potential, and that the way to get closer to this vision is through youth leadership. The activities varied from taking part in exchange programs to taking a role in the operational management of the organization. It might sound a little complicated but, in general, AIESEC acts as a platform to empower and equip young people, through their actual experiences, to bring solutions to the world's problems. These solutions could be as simple as being better individuals in everything they do in their society, or as complex as anything that you might imagine. I could go on for days, or weeks, listing and describing all the developments and realizations I experienced during my time in AIESEC but that is not the main objective of this book.

The organization is not perfect. It keeps evolving constantly, just as the management team changes every year while the young people who run it keep developing themselves through the process of learning by doing. So, mistakes were often inevitable. But, apart from my being able to explore a collection of management skills and the entrepreneurial mindset, leading the organization at a national level brought an intense wave of growth in my self-development, understanding, and character building.

Being entrusted with the responsibility of managing the national operations of AIESEC in Indonesia unexpectedly bestowed upon my dreams a new hope. Seeing the ambitious eyes and sensing the pure hearts of young people from different cities across Indonesia, each of them acting for the good of the nation, showed me the possibility of a much better future. Leading AIESEC in Cambodia, and living independently in a country I had never visited before expanded my worldview and my perspectives on different cultures, while deepening my understanding of myself and my personal values.

My experience working in this not-for-profit organization as a young adult was remarkable. To some extent, it was life changing. Having the privilege to interact with thousands of brilliant young people from different parts of the world opened my eyes to what their true power is when they have a strong Purpose.

While I was actively involved in the organization I had started initiating positive change by developing other people: instilling in thousands of young people a belief in the possibility of a better future for one's nation. Eventually I came to understand, the fact I was able to do that in my early twenties meant I didn't need to wait until I turned forty or fifty to make a difference. And, it all started one day when I randomly decided to take part in a student organization. It made me understand it was never too early to trigger positive change and that I should start as soon as possible.

You may have had a similar or a completely different experience. You may have had previous adventures but haven't yet realized how powerful the lessons you gained from them are, or you may not have had any eye opening experiences at all up to now. It doesn't matter. What matters is whether you want to start; because it is never too late, and it is never too early to begin. With this book in your hands, you can start now.

Why I Do What I Do

I told you at the very beginning I have a selfish reason here, and I don't want to play any tricks to brainwash anyone for the sake of business. I want to be an 'open book' and tell you what my real objective is. Before I elaborate on the reason why I do what I do, I would like to introduce you to a good friend of mine so you can get to know *his* reason. Let's call this friend, Alan.

Alan has been building his own business for the past three years. He and his partner run a consultancy firm promoting positive culture in companies and organizations as well as providing support for individuals to become their best selves.

The ideas and planning for his current business were concretely developed around 2013, but Alan had the desire to do this work since long before then. According to him, he sees what he is doing as being his responsibility to contribute toward improving the world's condition.

As any entrepreneur would say, the road of entrepreneurship is challenging and dynamic. No one can guarantee when, and whether or not, a start-up will succeed or go bankrupt. Alan didn't actually get any personal income for the first two years but, as he puts it: "I generally feel that this journey has been exhilarating! It is tough and scary but it's exciting. I also realized that this is a never ending journey and commitment, but this is worth it and has been really fulfilling". Ah, and have I told you that he's one of the most positive people I've ever met?

Before you start thinking I'm promoting an entrepreneurial lifestyle here, I'd like to clarify one thing: I happen to know a lot of happy and fulfilled employees as well as some negative entrepreneurs. My reasons for writing this book are not to motivate everyone to be an entrepreneur. I personally believe the entrepreneurial journey is not really for everyone, and it is not the ultimate key to fulfillment in life. But, in Alan's case, it was.

Consider what Alan's schedule looks like every day. He lives in a city with one of the worst traffic situations in the world. Thus, he needs to leave home at 7 a.m. every morning so he can drive his car through traffic for 90 minutes or more. He then works from 9 a.m. to 6 p.m. After work, he gets back into his car and drives through unbearable traffic once again to get home. He arrives at approximately 8 p.m. and he'll do it all again the next morning. After living in the city for several years, he has accepted the horrible traffic as an inevitable reality. I know that his daily schedule is not actually any different from other 9-5 corporate employees.

I remember when my life revolved around the same traffic-ridden city. It was always interesting to hear the blabbing of urban workers in malls or while riding public transportation. I could sense the frustrations of these people through their stories: their tales of being drained by their day-to-day jobs. On the surface they all have different reasons, but underneath they are all similar. This isn't the case with Alan. Somehow, he is able to look at his 14-hour schedule—potentially lasting the next 30 years of his life—differently. It seems he has an invisible force that drives him, imbuing him with positive energy even when he faces challenges. And that force flows through him and into his surroundings.

People like Alan have been an inspiration for me while working on this book. Lately, I have been exploring a concept called 'Ubuntu', which is an old African saying that literally means, 'I am because *YOU* are'. I am at my best when you are at your best. It also means human beings inevitably have a connection with each other.

You are influenced by the people closest to you and you also influence those surrounding you. What people think, feel, and do as well as how closely they are connected to each other on a daily basis determines their best selves. When you are at your best, you also provide support for your surroundings to be their best. Therefore, making the world a better place starts from ourselves. It starts with you, and then it snowballs from there.

Knowing how important it is to be at our best, you may want to know how to be at your best so that you can have a radiant energy that spreads to others. On average, people spend 50 – 63% of their total waking hours working, which adds up to more than 96,000 working hours over a lifetime. Simply put, work is taking up a huge space in our lives, and what we do to fill that space affects the personal aspects of our general life condition. One would think such a large part of our lives should be an incredible experience but the ugly truth is that "most people—80% according to Deloitte's Shift Index survey—are dissatisfied with their jobs," says Alyson Shontell in her October 4, 2010 *Business Insider* article.

Workers can dislike or even hate their jobs for various reasons. It could be due to a disengaged company culture, underpayment, the duration of their commute, or being led by a difficult boss. Aside from any external factors, the strongest root cause of dissatisfaction is internal.

Not long ago I was having coffee with an old friend who was working for a well-known multi-national company. We talked about this particular phenomenon and, surprisingly, he later admitted he was one of the 80% of the population who are dissatisfied with their work.

He told me how he didn't feel fulfilled in his job and actually hated his company's continual harm to society. At the end of our afternoon chat he spoke candidly: "What's the point of making the company bigger and more profitable only to help the rich get richer?" He had massive anxiety over the fundamental question of 'Why do I do this?'

Now, back to Alan. He also asks himself that same fundamental question. Alan's life is far from easy: he faces many challenges in his career and personal life and carries various fears and worries just like any other human being. But, there's something about him that always seems positive and alive. He has the belief that, as a citizen of this world, he has a duty to take part in shaping its future. No matter how large or small, he wants to take action toward building a better tomorrow. He consciously chooses his role. It grounds him in every step he takes because he knows the core reasons why he is doing what he does.

Alan states that he and his team truly believe in what they are doing. They actually believe in their cause, the foundation of which is: 'Why do we do what we do? This is more than enough to keep him positive. He admits that from the very beginning of his entrepreneurial journey he has known the road would be difficult. He has always been prepared for tough moments, though he doesn't know what form those challenges might take.

The future is unknown but, because he is driven by Purpose, he chooses to embrace it, all the while believing that the universe will always provide unexpected ways to help him. Those who know him consider him lucky, but he knows there's no such thing as luck or accidents. He meets his ups and the downs as everyone does, but he believes the universe will show him the way.

No one has ever properly and accurately assessed if Alan is happier than the rest of society but there is a different kind of energy that he transfers to his surroundings. He subconsciously instills optimism, positivity, and energy to move forward in his surroundings. He is grateful and excited for the challenge. I know well enough that energy cannot lie, it is the reflection of your one true soul.

People who love what they do for a living bring positive energy to their surroundings. They perform better and they develop a nature of continual exploration and learning. They are driven by strong reasoning and determination. They know they are part of a bigger picture. Thus, they consciously take a role in improving their environmental conditions. Furthermore, parents fulfilled in their careers create positive environments to raise their children in, which in turn creates a better future for generations of people. This can be expressed in a simple formula:

"The more people love what they do
and the more they feel spiritually fulfilled with their careers,
the better the world will become to live in."

I felt more alive than ever when I realized I was part of a bigger picture. From my Independence Day turning point years ago up to now, life has been one crazy adventure after another in endless succession filling me with a substantial sense of meaning and Purpose. The moment

I realized everyone is born for a reason, I started looking at my life differently. And, I've been living my life differently. I have evolved from being a complainer with a victimized mindset, feeling stuck in a broken society, into a conscious citizen who wants to take charge and find a way to contribute toward making the world a better place.

I know the reason for my existence and the role I play in helping others. I love the sense of fulfillment I get from supporting other people and helping them to unleash their potential. I know how wonderful it is to fulfill the reason for my existence, especially while making an actual living doing it. I know the delightful feeling of being driven by a clear Purpose.

This whole journey, from my awakening 'slap in the face' to the opening of unexpected doors, has shown me that it is never too early—or too late—to start contributing. This has led me to fortuitous meetings with a variety of people along the way and guided me to extraordinary and purposeful individuals like Alan.

Finally, it has led to my discovering and strengthening my own Purpose of enabling other people and helping them to understand themselves better and, ultimately, to realize their *own* Purpose in designing and living a purposeful career.

This is what now drives me and forms the foundational framework of my own career path.

This is how it begins…

"Some people die at 25 and aren't buried until 75."

(Unknown)

Chapter 2

Finding Your Self

We've had a glimpse of how Purpose plays a role in our lives and now we can start delving into the process of discovering Purpose.

It is not a one-size-fits-all solution. The process of discovering Purpose differs from one individual to the next. One person may achieve clarity from a single significant event, while another may need years to perceive it, and some people may never find it at all—hopefully, that doesn't apply to you. One thing that really helps in the process of finding one's Purpose is to consciously and continually engage in conversations with your inner self. Get to know who you are on the inside. This should be easy, but our noisy world can turn this task into a challenge.

Many people find it difficult to be in complete solitude on a daily basis. Even when we think we are alone, as long as our smart phones are at hand, we are in constant connection with the virtual world. From the moment we wake up until the time we close our eyes in slumber we are surrounded by noise. This noise can take different forms, be it our relatives telling us what to do with our lives or a social media status telling us what is 'normal' or 'great'.

It's just too easy for us Millennials to be trapped in both the virtual world and our social frameworks. The activities and/or achievements of the social circles we follow online can build one definition of societal success, which in turn can pervert our own personal idea of success and happiness. For example, sometimes we will allocate a certain budget for our travel to new and beautiful places just so we can post wonderful pictures to our Instagram, often to the extent that we neglect basic necessities.

We often tend to pursue things we think we need, but we don't actually need them. It is easier for us to listen to a crowd of external voices instead of our own singular, internal one. Therefore, this book has been created to help you through these challenges and enable you to have a deeper understanding of yourself. It is intended to drag you out of your busy routine for a few minutes every now and then, to turn down the volume of the external voices, and to make the world a better place by guiding you on YOUR purposeful journey.

The Power of Listening

Since 2009 I have been participating in various facilitation programs for young people. My Passion for facilitation arose when I realized how the process would always bring me positive energy, especially when it unleashed the potential in other people, enabling them to understand themselves better as well as bringing them closer to being their best selves.

It's no secret that, for a facilitator to succeed, they need to listen attentively: not just to hear the words but to listen with their hearts to discern what is behind the words being spoken. Deep listening is a core way to ensure that one understands the person in front of you, without being distracted by one's initial judgment. In any facilitation process, the facilitator or coach may not always give feedback or suggestions. Most of the time they will focus on asking the right questions, giving their clients space to listen to themselves. The facilitator will listen to what they are saying about themselves as well as to other bits of information that will give them clues as to who their clients really are. A crucial turning point comes when a client begins peeling off past assumptions about themselves and starts digging deeper into their inner being.

Whether we realize it or not our brains are always geared to find answers when faced with a question. Most of the time though, since we live in a noisy world and are part of the lives and thoughts of others, our natural capacity to dig deep and listen to our true self is weakened. Our assumptions and beliefs are formed by our past experiences and, sometimes, by other people's beliefs. A good facilitation process, involving the right questions, will give the soul a safe environment to be fully present and give us the courage to view our experiences from a new perspective.

This leads to the discovery of the one true self, which often doesn't happen in a single significant moment. Usually a person will go through a process of connecting dots on a map until they find their treasure: a greater understanding of themselves.

This self-discovery is fundamental. It will lead us further towards the correct path and unleash our potential. Once someone has discovered themselves without dark clouds covering the truth—seeing themselves so clearly they cannot resist it—there is no way to go back to wearing their old masks or choosing a direction they're not supposed to go in.

In my journey facilitating others, I am often reminded we need clarity—of ourselves, of our minds and of our souls—to listen with our hearts. And, more importantly, we need to listen to ourselves.

Training ourselves to be more aware of our inner responses can be an immersive process. We often need to build this awareness slowly, just like changing a habit. We can shift from a habit of listening too much to the external opinions that surround us, to a habit of listening to our true selves. There are many ways to sharpen our 'listening skills', some more effective than others. There are methods you can train yourself for, such as having a ritual quiet time in the morning, engaging in expressive writing, keeping a journal, taking a full day away from mobile devices, and meditation.

Meditation doesn't necessarily mean we have to close our eyes, stay silent, and keep our minds empty for hours. What we want to focus on during meditation is the management and awareness of our breathing which will allow us to achieve a calm state. This provides a special clarity to our thinking. It is a chance for us to push the pause button and see our circumstances clearly from a perspective of serenity; to have a conversation with ourselves and get some distance between us and our daily autopilot.

When we meditate we act as an observer of ourselves and can become an interviewer, asking ourselves the right questions. This process can be done in the lotus position, lying down, or in any way that suits you such as dancing, walking, or even while hitting the treadmill. I personally do this process most often through my writing and I love it.

For several years I have been journaling, capturing new insights from my personal experiences and having open conversations with my inner self. The type of questions I ask myself are usually simple, such as "Hi, what's in your head right now?", or "How do you feel? What made you feel that way?" I allocate a specific time each day to journaling and the results have been incredible.

Since it is intended to be a personal journal, I allow myself to do free flow writing without thinking too much. I can therefore skip the editing process and that allows me to just keep on going until I feel there's nothing left to write. This method has been especially helpful in facing personal challenges. When I feel negative, when I feel like there's no solution, I write. After writing down all the uneasy yet honest thoughts in my head, I close the process with a constructive question, such as "What can you do to make it better?

When I start journaling by asking a question, as I do when I facilitate with others, I allow a safe space for soul-digging and provide precious time to be completely honest with myself. It helps me to see issues from different perspectives, eventually finding reconciliation. Journaling also helps me build a strong bond with my inner self, creating a deeper level of understanding. This process enables me to connect the intelligence of the head, the intelligence of the heart, and the intelligence of the body—all through the work of my hand.

However, if we spend too much time with other people's thoughts in our heads we can have a difficult time hearing our own inner voice, almost as if it was nearly muted. Thus, I try to do this process as regularly as possible. Journaling is the core method we will work with in this book. It will be an ongoing exercise in listening to yourself, while also teaching you to silence the external noises that surround you.

Your Double Roles

As I mentioned earlier, you will be writing and creating as you move through the pages of this book. It will be an exercise encouraging communication with your inner self, causing you to take a double role: not just as the reader, but also as an active creator.

Pause for a minute. I'd like to invite you to experience a first short journey in creativity.

> In your own words and in your own way,
> describe how you see yourself on a piece of paper.
> You may write a paragraph, a poem, a song, sketch or
> drawing, attaching pictures and words from magazines, etc.
> Basically, do anything you feel like doing to explain,
>
> **'How you see yourself'**

Through the act of creating, by using your own hands, you have space to express yourself freely and completely; you are free from having to follow any standardized definitions. It is well known that art (including writing) usually involves certain imaginative skills and has countless different purposes. One of the purposes of art is to embrace the expression of thought, imagination, and emotion: aspects that arise from the human needs of balance and tranquility. Another purpose is to be a communication tool, connecting you to your inner self and to others across cultures and generations.

This book is all about you. The stories and explanations I share in the following chapters serve only as brief guidance, while at the core of this book are the activities you will experience. There will be questions and instructions at the end of every chapter, as well as on 'special' pages, that will help you along the process of discovering yourself, understanding your Purpose, and envisioning and designing your own purposeful career.

It is crucial for you to be honest with yourself along the way, to start dividing and understanding which of your beliefs are actually your own and which come from external— society's, or other people's—perceptions. This book is yours, you are free to do whatever your soul wants you to do with it. You may keep it confidential or you may share your experiences with those close to you. People you trust can be a great supporter of your personal growth.

To every activity an approximate time for completion is given, but this is only a guideline—not a time-limit—and is provided to help you plan ahead. For most activities, you are advised to be focused and free from distractions; this is because it is best if the activities are finished in one go instead of being stopped and then resumed. Focus and continuation play an important role in ensuring your flow and providing a special time for you and your soul. Space and time are created to drag you out of your autopiloted, day-to-day routine, to spend quality time alone with your own mind and emotions. The questions and guidance in this book will ask you to create conversations with yourself. Imagine you are the interviewer interviewing yourself. Take a little distance to see objectively, and understand, your true self.

In our world full of noise, it is important for us to be present in the 'here and now', to consciously pause our routines and responsibilities and be completely present, to give our souls the privilege of being heard. Tune out the noise, including social media, and sharpen your senses and your capability to acknowledge and classify your own emotions in the process of understanding yourself better.

Why Ask Why?

(originally published on https://medium.com/the-intersection-project)

It was a rare, chilly afternoon in Bali. I was in my regular corner, with my legs folded on a couch, in my favorite coffee shop where I was allowed (at least I assumed so, since no one had ever told me otherwise) to use the seat cushion of another chair as my personal table so my laptop could sit comfortably on my lap.

I found myself stuck, unable to continue my writing. It had been four months since I had laid down the first page of my non-fiction book. The fun, and creative writing part, of the process was over. My writing partner, Puri Lestari, and I had been continuing the Book Project, engaged in a systematic rewrite for quite some time.

I knew in my heart that, once the tap stops flowing, drinking gallons of caffeine won't release the next paragraph. What I usually do to fix such an uncomfortable condition is grab a blank piece of paper (a huge one) and start doing a quick mind-mapping process with coloured markers to peel away the complication in my head. Sadly, I hadn't brought my 'weapons' with me to the coffee shop that day, so I decided to take a short break and send a quick text to a friend in Seoul.

Separated, as we are, by thousands of miles, our friendship is far from just hanging out in a restaurant or going to have a manicure together. We connect through conversations and intense discussions that are often triggered by something abstract; and these conversations lead us into new adventures and the discovery of some new understanding. That particular afternoon we had a very exciting discussion over virtual space, after the day's gossip was finished, of course.

One thing I find fascinating about my friend is her ability to throw out the right questions when I need them most. When I share my complications and roadblocks with her she almost never gives me suggestions, instead she listens intently. Then, after my endless, random speech is over, she will pose a single, simple question. Most times I am surprised by the answers I give her. It's like I have been trying to find a needle in a haystack, but the needle was always actually in front of my face. It's one of those mind-blowing, 'oh-my-God-I-didn't-know-it-has-always-been-there' moments.

On that particular day, I told her my desire was to be surrounded by more people with her super-powers. I believe that the ability to suspend our opinions and ask the right questions is a kind of wisdom. We discussed the privilege human beings have of being able to explore newer and greater understanding, and of their feeling enlightened by their findings.

There is something innate about wanting to give people direct answers to their complex problems. Maybe it's human nature to compete: an inner desire that says "I should be able to finish that crazy puzzle" or that wants to be the best. Even when we care about another person we can forget to listen and, instead, provide our own moral opinion as a cure-all before we get all the information.

This problem is deep-rooted in our academic system, reinforced by years of questions with only black-and-white answers. A test is given with rigid, key answers and it limits the explorative ability of students. Because of these years of conditioning we busy ourselves looking for the 'correct' answers to questions rather than enjoying the mystery of exploring both the variety of possible answers and the new questions those answers may pose. We forget to let other people 'listen' to themselves.

It is very important that we keep curiosity alive when questioning others, but it is even more important to keep curiosity alive in questioning ourselves. Just as it is important to spend quality time with our loved ones, it is even more crucial to regularly spend time with ourselves. We should question and explore our authentic selves while learning to turn off external noise; or, at the very least, turn the volume down.

Toward the end of our conversation I could finally see a light at the end of the tunnel. Our random discussion, as usual, had led me to a new level of understanding and had served as a reminder of the importance of curiosity. My tap was unblocked and it was time to fill pages with words again. Before typing, however, I decided to turn off my mobile phone for a while and spend some time with my muse.

1st Special Page

Intention and Expectation Setting

By continuing to hold this book in your hand, I believe you have understood the reason why it was created and how it can assist you throughout the journey of discovering and knowing yourself more deeply.

In order for us to continue our journey together in the right way, it is crucial for you to understand your own intentions and expectations. Feel free to come back to this page at any time to remind yourself why you are here.

Estimated duration: 30 minutes
(including the suggested activity)

Remember, you may answer the questions in way you desire, and there are no limitations. You may write, draw, or use video, etc.

1. Who are you?

Try to describe your strengths, weaknesses, and also your personal views and perspectives on life in general, and other aspects such as love,
friendship, and career.

2. Get to know yourself on a deeper level.

Take the free online personality test at www.16personalities.com.
It takes approximately 15 minutes to complete.

Once you get your results, spend some time to read the explanation thoroughly. Try to compare it to your own description of yourself : your answer to question 1.

How relevant is the test result to your previous elaboration?

3. What brought you here ?

What were the reasons that made you want to read this book? How do you perceive your current personal condition in different aspects of your life?

4. What is your intention in taking this journey?

5. What is the single burning question
you really want to answer on this journey?

6. What obstacles, if any, do you see yourself
encountering during this journey?

7. What do you need in order for you
to be committed to this journey?

The journey of finding yourself is never going to be easy. The process might challenge your personal state, your current thoughts, beliefs, and points of view. All of these dynamics are crucial for you to understand your true self better than ever before and to help you pursue a fulfilling life. There will be temptations along the way to quit. In order for you to commit to yourself and achieve your personal expectations, it is suggested you write a letter of commitment to yourself.

The template below is provided as guidance. Feel free to write it in your own way. You can always go back and re-read your letter whenever necessary as a reminder of why you are following this process.

Dear _____
(your name)

    I think it is important for you to go through the whole process of understanding yourself better because

_____

_____

_____

_____

    Throughout the journey, I expect you will find crucial answers, especially in the areas of

_____

_____

_____

_____

    In order for you to achieve your expectations (and beyond that), you must be committed to keeping an open mind throughout this process and follow the journey to its end. Whenever you feel challenged, remember to be solution oriented, trust yourself and be grateful because it means you are in the process of growth.

    Congratulations for taking this courageous first step, I hope you enjoy the journey

Sincerely,

_____
(your name)

_____
(current date)

Chapter 3

A Purposeful Career - A Fulfilling Life

Every person deserves happiness. Period. This thought has been roaming around in my head for as long as I can remember. There was even a time when I firmly stated that happiness was one of my personal values. Along the way I became distracted, but eventually I found my way back to the path. I have always subconsciously observed my surroundings (as well as myself) to look for factors that contribute to the creation of inner happiness.

There were times, I remember, hanging out with friends in a café, when I found myself asking one particular question between the laughter and conversations:

"Am I happy?"

Whenever the question popped up—at that very moment—I came to understand that I wasn't happy.

Joy can come from simple things. You can feel positive and joyful whenever you smell a bouquet of roses, or when you laugh out loud with your best friends, or when you have dinner with your family, or when you take the first bite of your favorite food, or that beautiful feeling from a first kiss or the next thousand kisses from your significant other. Joy can be found in little things. But, what about happiness?

There is a more sustainable positive energy that can drive one out of bed and into the world every morning. More than just a series of joyful moments, happiness is a state of well-being. It is the sense of contentment that comes from within. It signals you are doing something meaningful and exciting.

Happiness is a combination of fear and excitement, gratitude and challenge, filled with determination. A determination coupled with the feeling of honor in knowing you are trusted to have a role and deliver a responsibility. Happiness comes from understanding that your life has a particular reason. It has a Purpose.

Purpose vs Destination

A Purpose isn't the same as 'a goal'. When we think about a Purpose, we often mistakenly consider what our life goals should be, or what we aim to achieve. People think about the 'end' of the journey; but the 'finish line' is not actually the Purpose, it is the destination. Purpose is there in the beginning and throughout the entire journey.

Marathon running has become a trend in my circle of friends and I support this new lifestyle. It is far from easy but lots of people still want to do it. Here is how it goes: a person can run for hours in a marathon. Reaching the finish line can indeed be a strong motivation. However, no one I know who has actually been in a marathon has ever taken reaching the finish line as their main reason for running one. Some said their main reason is to get healthier, to train, build endurance, find self-actualization, and to feel the huge positive energy that comes after they finish it.

Every marathon runner knows that, in order to complete the run, they need a lot of preparation. They know why they want to continue the long journey and how to enjoy the process. For my marathon runner friends, their destination is the finish line, but their Purpose is to run. To do the complete tough preparation is a combination of becoming fit, building endurance, and experiencing positivity and the rush of adrenaline. Destination is the goal. Purpose is the reason we head towards a destination in the first place.

This applies to careers and life as well as marathons. While goals can motivate you along your journey and make you feel great the moment you achieve them, what makes you feel even more alive and keeps you happy in the ongoing and endless process, is when you know the reason why you choose to do it.

Destination is the end goal you want to achieve in something you do or you choose to do, while Purpose is the main reason for one's existence, or why someone has this strong desire to do something. Destination can be formed by one single dot, while Purpose fills the whole line of your process.

Purpose fills the line of process towards your Destination

Regardless of what you believe in or what you think about life after death, one thing we know for sure is that the finish line of every human being's life 'marathon', is death. But, what is the Purpose of one's existence? What do you want to leave behind, after reaching your destination on this earth? That would be an interesting answer to discover, if you haven't found it yet.

No matter how long one's life is,
in the end it would be represented by that
one short line between 2 numbers.

What is my Purpose to take this whole journey?

How do I want to fill that line?
What do I want to leave behind?

In Loving
Memory

1989 — 2089

Why a Purposeful Career?

Life is full of problems and challenges. This is definitely not new information and it will always be that way. Yet, there are countless people who wish life were simple and ideal. I was—and sometimes still am—part of that group. The moment we acknowledge and accept that life is challenging is the moment we can finally stop asking, "Why is this happening?" and focus, instead, on solutions.

Another way of seeing these challenges in a new perspective is not only to accept that it has happened, but also to be grateful for what has happened. I believe everything happens for a reason that we will only be able to understand in the future when we look back and connect the dots. Some people are normally able to see the silver lining in challenging situations. But, there are more difficult moments when one is surrounded by fears: of the uncertain future and of one's own capacity. Try looking at your surroundings. It is not difficult to meet unhappy people who complain a lot, and their complaints are manifestations of the subconscious expression of their worries and anxiety.

People in their 20s and early 30s have many names to describe the phase of life they have the privilege of experiencing: e.g. 'quarter life crisis', 'self-discovery', and 'the start of adulthood'. Whatever the name, we can agree this phase is uncomfortable and confusing. It's when we come to know we are not kids anymore.

Changes and adaptations are inevitable in our social lives and we learn that even our closest friends will choose a way to live their lives that differs from ours. We begin to acknowledge the questions, sometimes unspeakable, that everyone has. A soft voice speaks in the back of our mind continually, asking what we've been doing all this time, asking about the future, asking about happiness, asking about relationships, asking about ourselves. This is a time where we face choices knowing that each decision will affect the rest of our story. If you hear that voice in the back of your mind, be grateful for two reasons: first, because it is one of the signs of growth, and second, because it leads you into a journey of finding answers.

This critical time in life comes with one of the crucial choices: What career does one want to pursue? It has always been a non-stop discussion over coffee, beer, lunch, dinner, or basically any time when we want to admit how it occupies our minds.

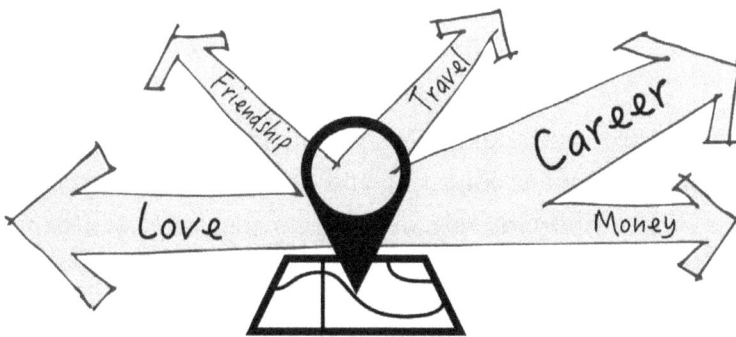

What do we know about career? We know that individuals, on average, work 50-63% of their total waking hours. We know that people often work more than 96,000 hours in their lifetime. We know for sure how those huge amounts of time can affect our happiness and health, but there is one thing we often forget: we forget that career isn't just measured in hours behind a desk. We often ignore that career is more than that.

Not everyone is aware there is a difference between a job and a career. A job can be something that is assigned to you, or you have assigned to yourself so you can get paid for it. A job may be defined by its title within the hierarchy of an organization, by its category in a list of job descriptions, or bound by a particular contract with a company. A job can be found in a list of openings on a website, a job fair, or any kind of open recruitment platform. This is not a career. A career is not like a meal you can choose from a list of foods in a menu.

The right career can only be found within yourself. No one else will know the answers but you. A career can be something that never existed before, that you may have created for yourself. A career is beyond what you are called by your bosses, or your subordinates. It is beyond a stipulated job description, and beyond the amount of time you spend in an office. Your career is what you choose to DO in life.

A career path can allow for more than one profession. It takes shape through diversity and over time. While it may have multiple connections, it is composed of a single theme. Your career may even lurk out of your sight because it doesn't match your primary job description; but you'll know it, because you have been doing it simultaneously the entire time. You might have been in the Sales Department and then assigned to Marketing Management, but what you have been doing that whole time is educating and developing other people. Our careers play an important role in bringing meaning, and happiness, into our lives.

PURPOSE

Twelve Things a 20-something Should Have

(originally published on https://medium.com/the-intersection-project)

No one ever says being twentysomething is easy. It can be scary. It can be weird and confusing. But, it can also be—and I'm sure it *must* be—very exciting.

Different voices say that by the time you reach twentysomething you should have achieved, and owned, various things. Especially during family gatherings and reunions there will always be some endless, and inevitable, questions about your life. They will come from all corners of the room.

In some cultures, being in your mid-twenties is the time for finding a soulmate and making babies. In others, it means you should have traveled to at least two different continents. In most societies, a promising career and financial sustainability should have been achieved before you leave your twenties.

How crazy does that sound? A few years ago you just celebrated the official legal age to drink or to drive. You have just tasted the sweet flavor of graduation. Then, all of a sudden, here you are, being expected to own all the complete pieces in the puzzle of the majestic picture called life.

Sometimes we want to see our future clearly, *right here and now*—tell me about it. We also want to have the ability to purchase a particular lifestyle. We are determined to give comfort and happiness to our parents and, of course, to our own selves. We are in need of traveling the world and we are craving for the public to recognize our achievements. Prioritization sounds like nonsense. We want *everything* on the list. All of them become the hot topic in any gathering and you are also bombarded by them in social media.

Everything seems to be *the priority*.

Just because we happen to see some posts from people we assume to be 'having it all' friends, we sometimes forget that:

1. Social media only shows the highlights of people's lives.

2. We have no idea what they actually had to go through and the sacrifices they have made.

3. There's *seriously* no such thing as a 'template' for living life.

Yet the list of social expectations—that eventually become our own expectations—on what we should have, can be endless.

However, there are some things that we *should* have during our twenties, of which we should remind ourselves:

1. The commitment to manage our health

It is not for us to live for as long as we can, but for us to be able to be in our best shape and be productive while we are alive.

A wise friend once told me that the top three nightmares for most parents are: if their children were to die before they do, if their children were unhappy with their lives, and if their children were to suffer from a sickness. So, if we want to make our parents happy, the simplest thing we can do is try to avoid these things.

2. The time for those people we care about and care about us

We may have thousands of friends around the world. We may meet new and interesting people every single day. We might not have the time to always have an ongoing conversation with all of our friends. But, it is indeed crucial to try our best to be in touch with the few people we care about the most and who care about us in the same way.

People will only know you care if they can feel—through your actions—that you do.

3. The time to regularly communicate with ourselves

There is only one particular person you should spend the rest of your life with, and there's no guarantee it need be your spouse or kids. Do you need any more reason why you should not regularly spend quality time—and have a conversation—with yourself?

4. The curiosity

This is the time for you to ask questions, and not always have the answer to everything. Being a twentysomething is the perfect time for you to take the wheel and continually get those 'aha' moments.

You have the energy and the time in your life. It is the best moment to explore the possibilities in life, to explore the world if you wish, to experience different things, and—most importantly—to explore yourself. It is the best time to start asking yourself: "Who are you?", and take the time to discover and construct the answer.

5. Understanding the roots of our fears

Knowing your ultimate fear is one thing, but understanding it is different. After acknowledging the existence of your fear and not hating yourself for having one (or two, or five), you also need to understand the reason for its existence or, in other words, *how* your fear was born.

You may have some initial fear—one that is constructed from a bad experience in the past—or a fear that is built upon external perceptions. Are you deeply scared of rejection, failure, or the fear of not being good enough? Understand how it was born. This is a crucial step you need to take in order for you to finally accept it, be at peace with it, and to choose courage instead.

6. The courage

If there's one thing we should experience in our twenties, it would be the thrill of starting something we've always been scared to do. Have the courage to follow your curiosity, actually *try* to give it time, and be surprised with the result.

Some say we should have the courage to start while we are young, without too many responsibilities, and when we haven't yet settled down. Well, I can't disagree with that. But what if, under some circumstances, a person has always had responsibilities? I prefer to say: *always* have the courage to do what you're afraid to do, *wisely*.

Do you want to do a solo backpacking trip? Do you want to try to that 'pixie' haircut? Do you want to remove some deep-rooted, toxic and negative people from around you? Do you want to start a new career? Take the step bravely but only if you're aware that every single decision will always have consequences. Have the right reasons to make that decision, and full awareness that you'll be ready to face the consequences.

By the way, if there are only two things we should experience in our twenties, I would say they should be the thrill in choosing courage and *the pain in experiencing failure*. That is the only way to learn fast: by always making *new* mistakes.

7. The ability and willingness to continually learn

There are always, *always* (repeat this word hundreds of times in your head) new things to learn.

8. The hope and perseverance

Expect things will be difficult. It will be crazy and challenging. There will always be circumstances that are inevitable and unexpected that will drag you down.

A two-in-one element that a twentysomething should always have is a combination of strong hope with even *stronger* perseverance. The speed of technological development offers instant processes that to some extent give us an illusion of how the general processes in life should be. But, do you know what else is instant? Junk food, one-night stands, corruption, and so on. You can make a list.

A meaningful journey with an honest process can *never* be instant. You need another level of stubbornness and hard work to make things work. It's difficult, challenging, and it feels endless. Take the time to enjoy the pain, because it means you're building your muscles.

That's how 'hope' takes an important role in your journey. While working your asses off, believe that the universe will conspire to help you out when you take the time to be persistent in trying to do what's right.

A clue to make things easier: surround yourselves with people who appreciate a long process of hard work. People who want instant success have a higher potential to stress you out.

9. The right attitude: ability to adapt and adjust

I can't stress enough how extremely crucial this point is for twentysomething individuals. For the past few years, we have probably learned how to plan and decide, only to discover we should always expect the unexpected. It is your adaptability in any kind of situation—while still holding on to your values—which will keep you moving forward, *not* your rigid plan.

10. Compassion and a heart to forgive

We are not grown-ups if we have never experienced any horrible pain in life. Pain gets even worse *not* just when it comes from our enemies. It is more difficult to comprehend when betrayal comes from people we trust the most.

Yet there are countless people who wish that life could be simpler and ideal (I was—and still sometimes am—part of that group). Once we acknowledge and accept the reality that life is indeed uneasy and challenging is the moment when things seem a bit easier. Once we understand pain is inevitable, we can finally stop asking, "Why did it happen?"

Only when we shift the driver of our feelings to the source of compassion, will we be able to accept, and eventually forgive, whatever it was that happened in the past. We should always have the heart to forgive others, and most importantly, *to forgive ourselves*.

11. Experience the art of being completely selfless

This can be a moment when you sincerely just give and expect nothing back. It might be that short volunteer project you take after your graduation. It might be as simple as helping a stranger who is in need. Experiencing a moment of being selfless will show you how to be selfish in the right way, because—guess what—thinking that you're doing something good for others will make you feel really, *really* good. Which leads us to the next point.

12. The desire to contribute something positive through what you do

Being in your twenties, you know you still have long winding years ahead you. If you're lucky, you'll still have around 30 to 40 productive years you can use for anything you would like to do.

We need to have the right reasons for choosing the direction of what we want to do in life. Given the fact we are bequeathed a lot of opportunities to grow, there must be a reason why we are so blessed.

Remember how nice it feels to help someone in need? Imagine how great it feels if you could contribute something positive through what you do during your productive years in life—especially if it can improve something you deeply care about.

We all have the chance to create stories to tell, and this may be just the perfect time to be aware of what our hearts want to contribute to them.

Chapter 4

The Journey of Discovering, Designing, and Living

When I started working in the non-corporate sector, I never actually thought about what my main reason was. I was simply amazed by the positive environment and the level of energy I experienced whenever we discussed how we could make a positive impact on society and, most importantly, by the strong feeling I got whenever I saw the impact we were actually making.

There were times when my friends and relatives asked me why I wanted to continue working in the organization when people my age had started getting corporate jobs right after graduation. They said something like, "Be careful, and don't start your *real* career too late. You need to be sure what company, and which position in the particular area you want to aim for. It takes time to get a promotion and to gain credibility."

I honestly considered all the things they told me, which did raise some concerns in the beginning. But, along the journey, I got an understanding of the real reason why I stayed and, finally, I could confidently answer those questions.

Before 2013, I had never lived abroad for a long period of time. And, on one election day, it was decided I would go to Cambodia all by myself for one whole year. Leading a team of nine people from six different nationalities—an operation involving hundreds of members of the organization—in a completely different society and culture was a challenge. At the same time, it was also a privilege. I was exposed to the reality of a different country that had a lot of potential for growth in the future, but one that also bore a deep misery shaped by years of past tragedies. I also came to understand how humanity is borderless and discovered true sincerity as the drive of my leadership—the main force that kept me going.

After finishing my one-year responsibility in that Kingdom of Wonder, I realized how exhausted I was. The experience was powerful, but it was also extremely dynamic and intense. So there I was, on the edge of making a decision: to continue striving for a better world or to seek a comfortable life by taking a safer road.

If you believe in God, as I do, you would believe that those who seek answers will find them. Right after my term in Cambodia, I had the chance to take a short trip to India. I was able to explore four different cities in eight days. I was in awe of the beautiful country and the richness of the culture, especially the architecture of the old forts, museums, mausoleums and temples. However, I was also struck by pain and intense emotions.

In one city, I could see homeless people every one hundred meters, wearing very little clothing, sleeping only on a piece of newspaper. There were children who could only take a shower whenever there was a downpour. And, don't even get me started on the condition of the babies I saw on the streets. I come from a developing country and poverty is not a new thing for me. However, seeing those stark realities right at the very moment when I was considering taking a more comfortable path really opened my eyes.

It was like the universe was telling me the answer to a question I didn't dare to ask. It seemed like it was telling me the world needs more fighters and that it didn't want to lose one of them. The problems may never be solved and the world may never be an ideal place to live, even up to the day I die; but that's exactly why the universe needs more fighters.

Fighting for a better world is an endless journey and I want to be part of the solution. That's when it hit me. Once you have clarity of Purpose, you can never run from it. That Purpose will keep reminding you why you're needed. That Purpose will find a way to keep you from getting lost in temptations.

The Endless Rollercoaster Ride

Living purposefully is not like climbing a mountain and reaching the top, where you wave your flag. It is a journey—long, endless, yet fulfilling—with nothing resembling a straight and easy path. A purposeful path would consist of multiple 'mountain-climbing' sectors: going to the top, celebrating the success, experiencing the downturn—fear and doubts, failures and hurt— just to have another moment of getting up once again after falling, and then climbing another mountain. Even after I thought I was clear about my Purpose, there were doubts along the way, especially when things got rough.

A few years ago I was part of a company called Insight Out. Working together in a dynamic team, we created 'I'm On My Way', a self-discovery and development program for young individuals across Indonesia. I was responsible for coordinating the curriculum designing process, project planning, and execution. At the start of the curriculum design I worked on, I got the chance to research and observe the journeys of various people who claimed they were living their dreams. They came from different backgrounds, areas, and sectors. From these observations, I noticed some strong similarities in their paths, which I tried to describe in the picture below.

Most of the time, their journey started from an uneasy feeling, or some persistent unanswered questions, about the condition of their existence. People have different experiences and signs at this stage.

This uneasy feeling, or the unanswered questions, can be exposed in a particularly dark moment or through a series of small events that lead us to 'Anxiety'.

In their early to mid-twenties (sometimes even earlier and, in rare cases, a bit later) young people are familiar with the symptoms of this particular stage, generally known as the 'quarter life crisis'. People respond to this condition in different ways. Some admit they actually take pleasure in this stage, enjoying the invisible confusion or discomfort. Others choose a method of temporary escape through self-help activities—meditation, yoga, traveling, or a scheduled hangout time—while thinking it may just be a normal phase everyone needs to experience, that it will eventually pass. However, some people have the courage to look for the ultimate answer.

Once you decide to strive for an answer—starting from that moment on—the journey becomes endless and dynamic. It will feel like a rollercoaster ride. It will give you an ongoing excitement and thrill. At any time, you might arrive in a dark tunnel full of challenges only to find some glimmer of hope, possibilities and tough lessons, with further surprises along the way.

At every stage of your purposeful journey, it is expected you will be exposed to unexpected circumstances. These will lead to a dynamic set of emotions. One thing for sure, this lifelong journey will require a high dose of positivity, courage, and excitement in learning endlessly, as well as persistence along the way.

You will be facing your own fears. You will be learning how to choose courage, every time. You will also realize that the process of building and shaping the necessary skills is endless and requires hard work. You will eventually learn that, in order for you to stay on track, it is crucial for you to have a support system.

The rest of your life will be an amazing—but definitely far from easy—path toward fulfilling your Purpose and getting closer to your vision. This is the continuing lifelong journey of discovering, designing, and living a purposeful path.

Discovering Purpose

The journey we are embarking on is intended to give insight regarding the right type of career one can have in life. The findings will cover both functions: the vehicle in which to live your Purpose *and* the way to make a living out of it.

As was mentioned in the previous chapter, one cannot find the answers by just reading this book. When we talk about 'discovering Purpose', you're the only one who can best tell what your Purpose is. This book is designed to facilitate your journey in discovering your Purpose by activating a conversation with your inner self, so that you can design your own career path based on Purpose.

There is no limit on the type of career we can pursue. Some of the most desired careers at the moment are not those predicted 20 years ago. They might have never even existed before. Therefore, the type of purposeful career you will pursue might probably be something not yet known in current society.

The upcoming process is all about being honest with yourself while having the freedom and courage to design what you feel truly aligned with. To start the journey of discovering Purpose, please look at the picture below:

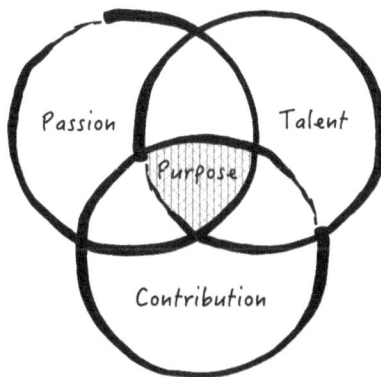

In the process of discovering Purpose, we need to explore the three big elements that ultimately formulate 'Purpose' in the intersection, which are:

1. Passion - what you really love to do
2. Talent - the potential you have, even if it has not been unleashed
3. Contribution - the part you desire to play that aligns with the needs of the world

We might have been familiar with one or all of these elements. We might understand the definition or we might already have some ideas on how these elements work in our daily life. But, what we will do together in this journey is to dig deeper and explore these elements within you. The journey is intended to enable a better understanding of yourself and to finally discover Purpose—or to provide a space for your Purpose to find you.

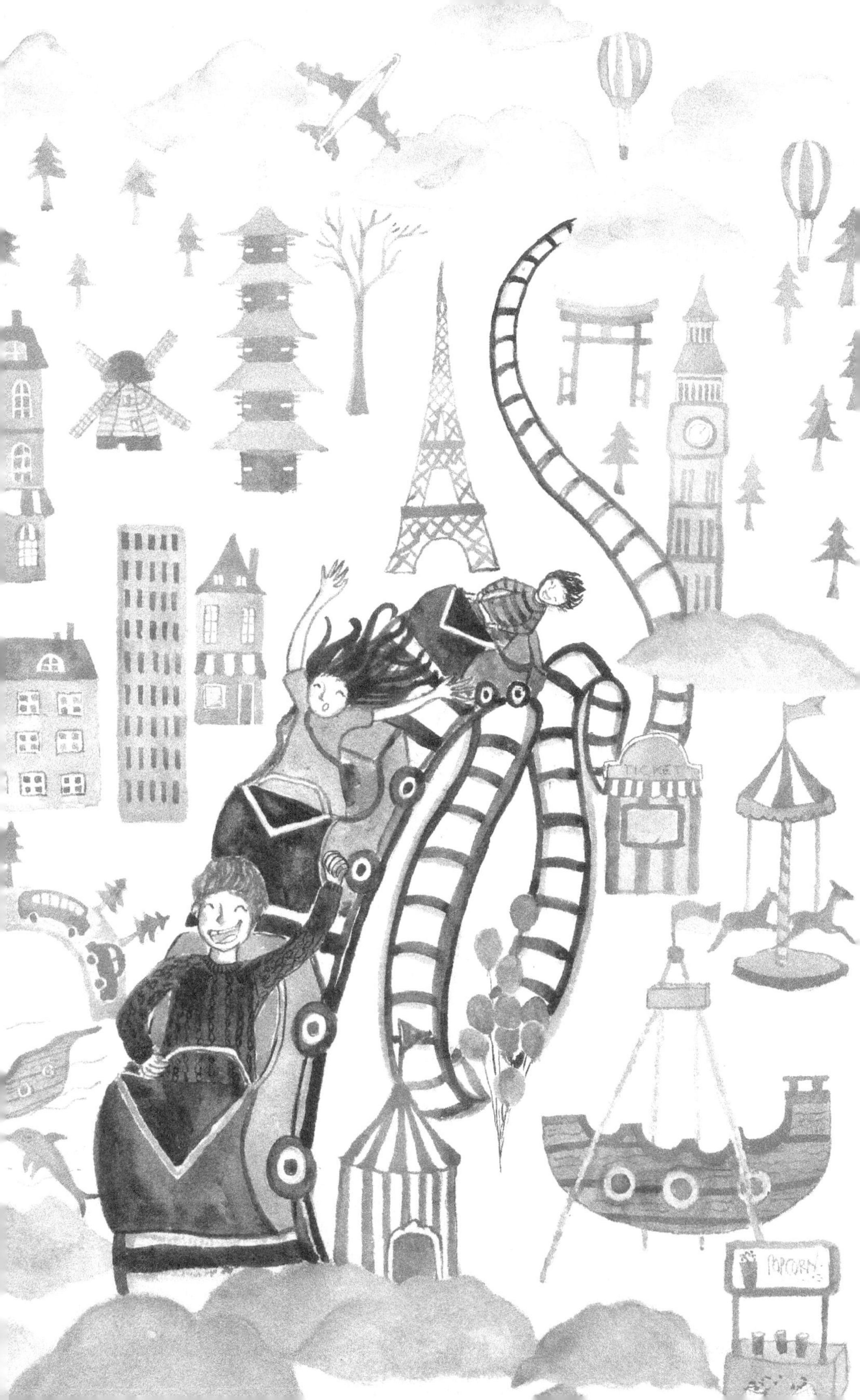
POPCORN!

2nd Special Page

Journaling

You have been briefly introduced to Purpose and why it matters. Let us pause for a moment and reflect back on the process so far. Try to describe your current honest thoughts, feelings, or assumptions on the previous chapters: 'A Purposeful Career', 'A Fulfilling Life', and 'The Journey of Discovering, Designing, and Living'.

Estimated duration: 10 minutes

Remember you may answer the questions in any way you desire and that there are no limitations.

---

1. What is in your mind, and what do you feel right now?

---

2. Do you have any doubts or concerns?

3. What excites you the most?

4. Take some time to turn back to the 1st Special Page'.

Re-read your intention and expectations.

Congratulations for the progress you've been making so far!

We will now go to the concrete process of exploring your Purpose.

Part 2

Exploring the Path to Purpose

"My momma always said,

'Life was like a box of chocolates.

You never know what you're gonna get' "

Forrest Gump (Forrest Gump, 1994)

Chapter 5

Do Not (Blindly) Follow Your Passion

I believe the word 'Passion' is probably not at all something new for you. Therefore, let us start in a different way.

Try to describe your answer to the question below, in your own keywords or phrases, in statements, drawings, photos, or poems. You can even sing, dance, or record a video—whatever you feel like doing to elaborate on the answer.

What does 'Passion' mean to you?

How did this short and simple activity make you feel? And, what was the main idea that came to your head when you first heard the word 'Passion'? Is it a hobby? An interest? Or, is it something you feel you're good at?

Through this previous exercise, what we want to further explore is the method you choose when you can freely do any activity you want. It is also for you to become aware of the type of emotion you feel when you do something you enjoy doing, because Passion is always strongly connected to human emotion.

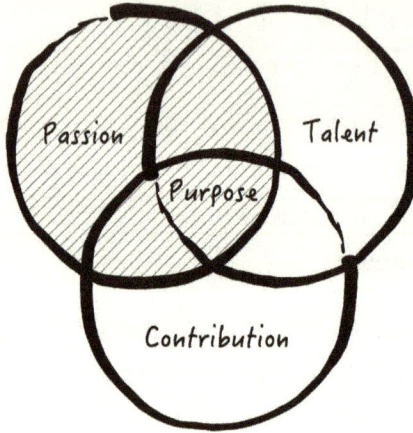

To put it in a simple statement, Passion can be defined as '*the thing you really love doing*'. It is not merely something you 'don't mind doing', or even just 'like doing'. It is something that you *love*. It is an activity that makes you feel excited and *ALIVE* when you're doing it. There is something in these type of activities that gives you pleasure and enthusiasm.

One of the most popular speeches of all time on Passion was by the iconic founder of Apple Inc., Steve Jobs. In June 2005, he delivered a commencement speech to Stanford's graduating class. He shared advice that was remarkable and reached across generations. He said: "You've got to find what you love…the only way to do great work is to love what you do. If you haven't found it yet, keep looking, and don't settle."

I could not agree more with his statement. People who love their jobs and careers, without any doubt, will also agree that Passion plays an important role in keeping them going. Passion helps you appreciate the process. It can also bring positive energy in difficult times.

However, is Passion the be-all and end-all?

In the past decade or so, there have been countless messages made to motivate Generation Y to follow their Passion, to be courageous and simply have faith in the notion that once you are brave enough to follow your Passion, money will soon follow. As someone who supports the importance of happiness in advancing your career, I must firmly state that such a message can be dangerously misleading. It's true you would experience joy if you could do what you love doing every single day. However, I have two main reasons why people should see Passion as only one of the factors to consider—not just the single invariable—in the foundation of your career decision.

First, Passion does not exist to be blindly followed. Recognizing your Passion can be a sign that you're able to do something great in life, and that's awesome! It can be a channel, or an important tool, in delivering your Purpose. However, just having Passion is not enough to get you to success and fulfillment. It needs to be complemented by other elements and obviously needs continual and endless hard work for you to be skillful in the area you're passionate about.

Second, and this is important, most people (if not all) don't just have *one* true Passion in life. Passion is not only those important activities and interests you can monetize. Passion can be found in small and simple things. If you are like me, there are a lot of things I do every day that make me feel alive and bring me unspeakable joy. So, how can we choose those particular Passions to be developed as a career?

Listening to the Calling to Choose a Passion

I have always known that I love to sing since I was a kid. I joined a vocal group when I was young for a brief period. I was also in a band in high school. Going from one studio to the next, winning some band competitions, performing on different stages with some talented young musicians were the highlights of my high school years.

While exploring my Passion for singing, I met different people who also had a Passion for music. Interacting with them—seeing how far they had come and how they gave their all to achieve their dream—made me question my intention of developing this as my future career.

For many reasons, I realized I didn't want singing to be my career, no matter how much I enjoyed it—and I still do. Or, perhaps, I knew another 'calling' was waiting for me. If that calling was strong enough, although it was a little late for me to start, I would still find a way to take it seriously.

Other things I consider as a Passion—something I love doing that makes me feel alive—are watching great movies or TV series (well, who doesn't love those things?), riding a bicycle, connecting with nature, traveling, and cooking. The list goes on and on.

Any kind of Passion can be developed into a great career. Some of my close friends have careers in the areas I have mentioned. As for me, I too eventually chose one particular Passion as the framework of my career. Now, I will tell you why, and how.

I remember the very first time I attended a youth leadership conference in 2009. I didn't know what to expect. As a passive participant, I just sat there, trying my best to pay attention to the speakers on stage. A lot of the sessions were delivered in a method I had rarely—if ever—experienced in any academic classes. They were not typical one-way lectures instilling knowledge via a rigid structure. Some of the sessions were delivered by asking questions, to enable delegates to explore what they saw, thought and genuinely felt. This method gave freedom to the participants to gain some realizations they did not have before: about themselves and their point of view on certain realities. That was how I was introduced to the art of facilitation.

It felt like I had been reading my life's journey in a book without noticing some important pages were stuck together. The process helped me become much more aware, and to open and read those hidden pages, giving me a whole new perspective. It brought a fresh point of view of how to perceive myself and my surroundings.

There were even some moments when I unexpectedly got teary-eyed from understanding how profound my realization was. It had transferred such intense emotions within me. Besides understanding the power of asking the right questions, I also explored how powerful a conversation could be.

There is a saying, 'sharing is caring', which I didn't fully understand until that conference. When participants explored their thoughts and feelings truthfully and genuinely shared their perspectives, and sometimes even their vulnerability, that's when human connections were established. When like-minded people are put together in one room, with a similar intention to openly share and listen attentively with compassion, the realizations and exploration of ideas could raise the roof.

Throughout the series of sessions, I got a better understanding of who I was. My perceptions evolved and I continued to believe that I, and other young people, could actually do something for this troubled world in a lot of ways. This realization was profound, and it stays within me still.

Along the way, I found some opportunities to become a facilitator. Even though public speaking was not my favorite thing, I was open to the challenge anyway. I remembered my teenage self, sitting in the hall and having a major revelation about my desire to contribute toward positive change. I wanted to be part of something bigger than myself. I wanted to help others to be transformed, just like I had been.

I was slowly exposed to the world of facilitation and became deeply fascinated by it. I was amazed by the thrill I got whenever I witnessed a person—or a group of people—discover something new about themselves and begin to explore their potential through the act of facilitation. I enjoyed the role of not ordering or forcing people to do something, but enabling them to find the right answers within themselves.

I love the feeling of contributing solutions to a problem (yes, this is also one of my Passions). I feel alive when I discover how one powerful question can bring many important answers and realizations to different people. I also find great joy whenever I realize how much I have grown through facilitating others in various programs. I am in love with the art of facilitation. And, this time, I do have a strong 'calling' for this Passion. This is what I'm meant to do. This is the Passion I'm meant to follow.

The Role of Passion in Living Your Purpose

There is a reason why Purpose needs to use Passion as a channel to deliver its objective. In most cases, the journey of living your Purpose, although it is very fulfilling, is far from easy. Challenges are there in different forms to either test you or scale up your capabilities. Failure will always be one of your best companions in the journey, although it can be painful and put you in a dilemma.

On a road less traveled, Passion plays the role of sparking the fun. Passion gives additional joy to the process of delivering your Purpose. It supports you by nudging you back into the field even when you know unexpected challenges are awaiting you. It's like playing your favorite sports or taking a dancing class in a gym: you know that exercise is important to keep you healthy and fit, while you enjoy the process because you love doing the activities. It's also like eating your favorite nutritious foods during meal times: you know that eating on time, and regularly, is crucial for your health, while you enjoy the process of managing your health more when you love the taste of your meal.

To understand and discover your Purpose, Passion is meant to be explored at the first level. This is the easiest and most basic element to discover, with little or no effort, because you do not really need to find it. There is no such thing as 'finding your Passion' because it is there all along. Your heart knows it well. However, what you *must* do is decide which one of your Passions can be a tool to fulfill your Purpose.

So far, two secrets have been revealed:

> 1. *Passion is not to be blindly followed, but should be used as a channel,*
>
> and
>
> 2. *Most people have multiple Passions in life. Therefore, it is impossible to turn all your Passions into a career.*

And now let me give you the third secret...

Passion May Continue to Evolve

It is true you don't need to *find* your Passion because it is already there all along. But, this doesn't mean that it will never change. I only discovered my Passion for facilitating in my early twenties. I didn't intentionally find it, it came naturally from circumstances in my life. I also didn't immediately love it. It took time for me to understand how it keeps my heart beating. Although the preparation can be wholly challenging, facilitating people always gives me indescribable fulfillment.

I just realized a new Passion lately. Truly, I had never imagined that at any moment in my life I would become a writer. I did like to write short notes, to journal, or to write secret poems, but I never had the courage or intention to take professional writing seriously. If I were able to tell my ten-year-old self she would write a book in the future, she would hide and lock herself in her bedroom. She would think I was crazy.

I have only been trying to write frequently over these past few months. I started writing mainly because I wanted to explore another method to facilitate more and more people without being bound by geographical limitations. I had no idea in the beginning how I would feel about writing. I was also a bit scared about the commitment I had to make. But, surprisingly, I love it. I feel a thrill when I open my laptop to continue writing. I experience great joy whenever I can deliver thoughts in words for people who need them.

Some people might have been aware of their ultimate Passion since they were little. Some people might have no idea what their Passion is, or they might have loads of them and are confused which Passion they want to follow. Others might still have the privilege to be able to explore and take an adventure to finally understand the right Passion to turn into a career—one that can bring them closer to the Purpose.

In any case, there's no need to worry, because every person has a different process and time scale. What's important is the willingness to attentively listen to your soul, to understand what gives you true joy. Because, while we are evolving, there is always a soft voice inside our heart. That soft voice has a desire to guide us. When we ignore it, or when we let external voices speak louder to us, the inner voice gets weaker. That's when we allow ourselves to be dragged down by external realities. That's when we let ourselves be driven by fear, rather than living on the meaningful path that we should be able to design and follow. But, when we pay attention, that inner voice will bring us closer to our Purpose. It has always been *our* choice to make. Do we want to listen to it?

Understanding the Essence of Passions

Our soul signals to us when we do something we love. It transfers joy, pleasure, and enthusiasm. What we need to do is understand the main driver of that positive energy and happiness. Those activities you particularly love doing all have something in common. Understanding the essence of your Passion can be the key to getting closer to the true nature of your purposeful career.

Certain people in a group may have a similar Passion for outdoor activities, such as running a marathon by the beach together, and yet the drivers of their pleasure might be different. One person enjoys it because it brings a sense of active physical movement. Another person derives pleasure from being able to connect to nature, while someone else is excited by the challenge of finishing an entire marathon.

A group of people in a band who love performing their music on stage also have various impulses. One person might feel alive for the sense of self-expression beyond words they get when they play a musical instrument, while others enjoy the pleasure, and appreciate the artistic magic, of the combination of different tunes from the many instruments and vocals. Another person might feel great compassion and happiness from their connection with the audience.

There are various essences of Passion that drive enthusiasm and pleasure within our soul. We need to know some of them in order to understand ourselves better. They are:

1. **Growth:** the pleasure that comes from the sense of improvement in your current state. This occurs in an enrichment activity when you get to explore new things and while learning: when you find

great joy in realizing you have improved a particular skill, are progressing in learning a new language, or are thrilled at discovering new information.

2. **Active movement:** when your excitement is derived from physical activities, when your muscles are flexed and stretched, when your sweat is dripping. Sitting down for hours behind a desk can be a struggle for you, while doing sports, mountain climbing, or dancing, may entertain your soul far more than winning a lottery.

3. **Connection:** this essence needs to involve two parties or more. You will feel alive and have a sense of happiness when you feel connected emotionally with other human beings, living creatures, and nature; or when you're spiritually connected with a higher power. It can be achieved through deep conversation, whether verbal or nonverbal.

4. **Expression:** can be found within people who otherwise find it difficult to open themselves to new acquaintances—who are reserved by nature. It resides in individuals who have a broad world inside themselves. They have various ideas and rich—sometimes overwhelming—abstract thoughts and emotions. Having a channel beyond mere words to express themselves will bring them a sense of joy and enlightenment.

5. **Creation:** the joy essentially driven by the sense of making something out of nothing, or forming a new thing out of raw materials. It involves creativity and innovation. It becomes pleasurable when you know you're able to produce or construct something that other people can use or consume.

6. **Challenge:** is in the adrenaline rush. It is the essence that comes from a sense of competition and is driven by the future reward of achievement. Sometimes it is not even necessary to have a real competitor. You can compete against your past self, or any common social perspective, to prove you are beyond whatever is thought to be a limitation.

7. **Art and Beauty:** a blending of emotion and a glimmer of mystery. It is about appreciating a combination of different variables in a new form, with a diverse possibility of interpretation. You find pleasure in the mix of colors, or lines and shapes, or words, or a medley of tunes. It's like entertaining your senses as they convert the input into certain emotions and thoughts.

8. **Relevance:** comes from the sense that you are able to provide an answer to a riddle, or that you are able to solve problems and offer improvements regarding certain issues or complications. You experience joy when you are able to provide the missing piece in a puzzle.

Explore Your Passions

We don't need to find Passion elsewhere. It is always there within ourselves. To end this chapter, I would like to invite you to communicate with your inner self in order to explore your true Passions.

 **Estimated duration:** 60 minutes.

Give yourself time to completely focus on yourself, without any distractions. Remember, you are allowed to answer the questions in any way possible (writing, drawing, painting, attaching images, mind-mapping etc.)

1. What are the activities you really love doing and that give your soul true joy and pleasure?

Instructions:

- Pay attention to these activities. Notice which of them you would gladly do even without anyone asking you to do so. It can be as simple as cutting onions, talking to your mother, hugging your friends, or riding a bicycle; or even some complicated or difficult pastimes like mountain climbing, or building a robot.
- Try to list as many as you want, as long as you are clear that these activities give joy to your soul.
- If you are still unsure, however, you may move directly to question no. 2.

2. When was the last time you felt ALIVE from something you did?

Instructions:

- Try to recall the moment when you were the *actor* in a situation. It was not something you just witnessed, or passively experienced. What was the moment and what did you do? What happened, and what was the process? How did you feel throughout the process?
- To make it easier, you could limit this exercise to a one-month period of your life. You might check some photos in your cellphone, in case you captured the strong, happy moment in a picture.
- Feel free to offer more than one moment.
- Remember to be completely honest.

Now, look at the list of Passions you just created. Assess them one by one and try to be specific :

1. What gives you joy?

2. What is it in an activity that drives the pleasure within you and gives you the feeling of being ALIVE?

Divide your answers into groups, according to the classification we have explored in 'Understanding the Essence of Passions'.

Here are some examples:

o If you wrote you like to 'run with friends in nature', what is the true happiness? Is it from the active movement you feel when you run? Is it from the human connection when you are having a good time with your loved ones? Or, is it because of the relationship you are having with nature?

o If you wrote you like to 'visit museums', what gives you that joy? Is it from the essence of growth and exploration as you are learning something new? Is it from the connection you feel with history? Is it from the expression of art and beauty you feel with your senses?

o If you have a Passion in 'writing poems', do you feel alive because it gives you the channel to express yourself in broad emotions? Is it because you can create something beautiful out of nothing? Is it the feeling of being spiritually connected to a higher power? Or, is it from the sense of understanding yourself better: learning more about yourself through writing?

Classify your responses and group similar answers into the following categories. Also, a Passion may fall into more than one single category. For example: the essential drivers for your Passion in dancing are both 'Active Movement' *and* a sense of 'Expression'.

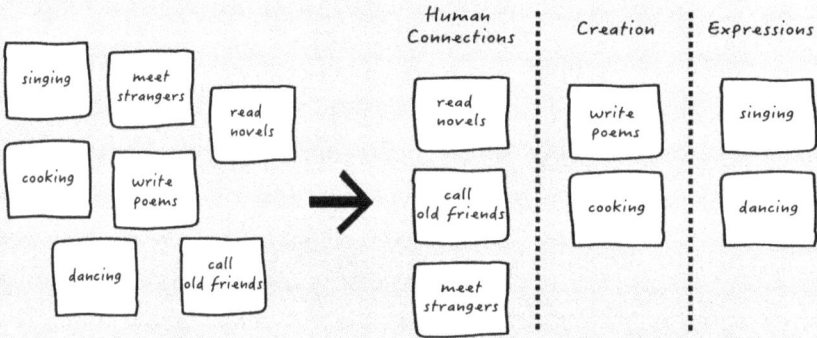

- **Growth**   - **Active movement**

- **Connection**   - **Expression**

- **Creation**   - **Challenge**

- **Art and Beauty**   - **Relevance**

- **Others***

*(If you have a Passion that does not fall into any of the preceding categories, feel free to suggest a theme that is relevant to you.)

What is your ultimate (top 3) group of Passions?

1. _____

2. _____

3. _____

After figuring out your group of Passions, I suggest you assess them further. If you have many different groups, try to prioritize them.

Why does your soul find joy in them?

From what you already know about yourself, take some time to reflect on what might be the reasons behind several of the Passions you have explored.

You may look back at the result of your personality test at the beginning of this book as a referral. For example, an introverted person finds joy in the essence of Expression because they feel they are better able to express themselves through art and music.

Note:

If you are still unsure about your true Passions, try to do fifteen minutes journaling every night before you sleep, for the next seven days. Try to observe in which moments you feel alive during the day. The feeling of being alive is sometimes not always experienced as a form of success or a simple joy. A challenging situation can also bring a sense of being alive; it can be a sign as well. Try to avoid asking other people. The best person you can have a conversation with about your Passion is your inner self. After finishing the seven days of journaling, you will have a better understanding of what activities your soul enjoys doing. With this understanding, you may then go back to tackle the activities in 'Exploring your Passion'.

Journaling

Congratulations on finishing the first set of activities in the chapter 'Do Not (Blindly) Follow Your Passion'. I hope you have enjoyed the process.

Now, please put aside around fifteen minutes to do a little journaling. You may respond to these questions in any way you like:

How was your journey in exploring your Passions?

How do you feel about the process so far?

What are the new realizations (or reconfirmations) you got from this chapter?

Is there anything new you just realized about yourself?

Do you still have any unanswered questions?

The Top 5 Wrong Reasons to Follow Your Passion

(originally published on https://medium.com/the-intersection-project)

In the past decade or so, there have been countless messages directed at motivating Generation Y to follow their Passion: to be courageous, and simply have faith that once they are brave enough to follow their Passion, the money will soon follow.

It's true that Passion can bring joy in life. However, if any of these following situations are your ultimate reason to quit your job and follow your Passion instead, then you might want to think further:

1. Because you just want to be your own boss

Following your Passion should never be defined as ultimately becoming an entrepreneur so you don't have to follow another person's orders.

Doing what you're passionate about *can* be done inside a corporate system while you're being led or supervised by another person. This means: even when you have followed your Passion, there are still possibilities of disengagement when you face a difficult boss, become trapped in a bad work culture, or are misaligned with a company's vision.

Second, even if your Passion is related to running your own business and becoming an entrepreneur, you will always have customers, and satisfying *them* matters in order for your business to grow. In a way, you still have a 'boss' in the form and shape of your customer.

By the way, even when we work for someone else, we can still be *the boss* of ourselves. It is crucial we know how to lead ourselves in any circumstance, whether as a superordinate, or subordinate. It is a matter of our attitude and behavior rather than our position.

2. So you don't feel like 'working' even for a minute of your life

Some people are driven to make a career out of their Passion so, to some extent, they might enjoy it so much they wouldn't feel like they were working at all. Some people say they want to have freedom of time and space so they can do less (perhaps only four hours a week) and have more time to enjoy life.

I happen to know a bunch of amazing people who work passionately at something they are doing. They love their job, and none of them has ever said they feel like *not* working. Exhaustion and frustration indeed exist in their dictionary, just as for any other normal human being. And, those of them who work independently—either as a freelancer, artist, writer, or entrepreneur—even admit they work harder and longer than nine-to-five corporate employees. As one of my (entrepreneur) friend's favorite quotes says: *'Entrepreneurs: people who work 80-hour weeks to avoid working 40-hour weeks.'*

Furthermore, the moment you start your own venture—unless you inherited a fortune from a very wealthy family—you realize that paying other people to do the jobs you don't like doing is not first on your list of investment priorities. There will be numerous other responsibilities—'not your cup of tea'—that you will still need to end up doing. You might need to do them long enough to realize how much you hate them and decide to hire another person to perform them. Or, you might just adapt and not mind doing them at all. Eventually, you may even start liking them, which brings us to the next point.

3. Because you think you wouldn't be happy doing anything else

Our generation has been fed too many talent shows beautifully packaged as so-called *reality shows*. While it's a guilty pleasure of mine to enjoy watching them from time to time, we definitely need to have a clear mind to distinguish what's *really* real from what has been spiced up—which might even create a new social reality.

One statement we've been hearing thousands of times in any talent competition is: "I couldn't imagine doing something else besides singing (or dancing, or cooking, or modeling)".

In today's world, we have come to believe that having a Passion is like finding a treasure, or one's true soulmate. It feels magical, like that 'we-see-a-unicorn-jumping-on-a-rainbow' kind of feeling. We have been made to believe that once we finally find it, we wouldn't be happy to do something else besides our Passion.

The truth is, while many people say they think they don't have any Passion, people can *actually* have more than one Passion. In fact, those who say they don't know what they're truly passionate about, might be in that dilemma because they already have too many things they enjoy doing. It's just that nothing stands out among the others.

4. To finally have a work-life balance for the rest of your life

'Being balanced' has no correlation with 'following your Passion'. There's no cause-and-effect relationship. These two phrases should never be forced to coexist in one sentence. A person who hates their job can be well-balanced in managing their time for sport, entertainment, and family, while also always meeting their deadlines.

Someone who makes a career out of their Passion—even if they had the freedom of time and space to work—might not *have time* to better manage different aspects of their life. They might tend to be overworked sometimes, or to work less other times; and the latter might make them feel so guilty they would work too much the next day leaving no time to do anything else.

If you're an independently located professional, being in your own bedroom 24/7 should also question the word 'balance'. Being balanced is a matter of prioritization and being committed to your plan. It is about consciously choosing balance, it is a commitment you should make and a skill you should practice *continually,* regardless of whether you like or dislike your job, whether you work for someone else, or just work for yourself.

5. Because you think you need to simply do what you love doing in order to have a happy life

Rather than chasing happiness through doing what you love, do something that would make you feel fulfilled, instead.

Even when you do the things you love, there are still a lot of difficult things in life you will face that will make you unhappy. Losing a family member, rejection, failure, a broken heart, sickness—these are some of the realities in life that can knock you to the ground. Even in doing an activity you're passionate about, there will come a time— after the honeymoon period is over—when your Passion will also feel like a *responsibility*, just like any other job would.

There is always a huge risk of failure and an endless road when 'starting over' in a career path. But, here's the secret. Simply doing what you like to do for a living won't give you a strong enough reason to get up again once things are freakishly difficult (*oh yeah, those toxic days would eventually come, no matter what*).

Apart from being crazily stubborn, what would help bring you back on track would not be the joy you find when you do the activity you love. As much as I find joy and pleasure in writing, there are days when my bed and blanket are far more pleasurable than opening my laptop and starting to type.

There are also lots of different circumstances that bring me down from time to time. What brings me back to my table every single day, is understanding the *reason* why I do what I do, not necessarily the activity I am doing. It is in perceiving the clarity of my reason or, as some will say: "*it is in the clarity of Purpose.*"

Chapter 6

A Seed Called Talent

Have you ever seen a five-year-old playing the piano so beautifully it left people awestruck? Or, listened to a singer and song writer in a talent show who has a unique vocal color and moving lyrics? Have you ever found yourself telling someone: "Wow, you are so talented in drawing!" This is the typical comment we make, or hear, when we compliment a performer or an artist. Other thoughts that might come to our heads are:

"Gee, how can a child perform so beautifully?"

"Since when did they start learning it?"

"They are really talented. They are gifted."

"I'm not talented. I would never be able to do that."

The term is definitely not strange to our ears: we keep hearing about Talent all the time in today's world. But, exactly what does Talent refer to? Does Talent only exist in the world of art? Is it true that some persons can be talented, while other people don't have any Talent at all? Do we know how to assess someone's Talent? And, more importantly, are we aware of our own Talent? These are fundamental questions that we are going to explore together in this chapter.

A lot of different perspectives and arguments arise in trying to see what Talent truly is. Some say it has a close connection with intelligence. Some say Talent and intelligence should be separated completely. Some people argue that, in the current generation, Talent is only seen as a potential that is related to art. Others say that a person can also be talented in an academic field. There are also discussions on how to measure a person's Talent, while other people say that Talent cannot be measured, it is only competency that can be assessed.

Talent is considered 'tricky' compared to the other two elements—Passion and Contribution. It might be something within us that isn't fully evolved. Therefore, it is not as visible and easy to recognize as a practical skill. Moreover, Talent also needs to involve an external perspective on how it is to be potentially developed to help us grow and excel at certain skills.

Validation of Passion and Contribution happens internally and *they* are driven by our hearts. We ought to know if Talent is right for our souls. Some people even take a professional psychological assessment to understand their Talent, while others—for example, parents assessing their children—would need to be fully aware and pay attention to certain symptoms and details. A person can say they have Passion in doing something, and no one can say that is invalid, but it doesn't guarantee they're talented in that area. One thing needs to be stated clearly here: every person has Talent. There are no exceptions.

Another reason why discussing Talent can be complicated is because, while everyone is able to pronounce the word, Talent is often misinterpreted. Before we move toward understanding precisely what Talent is, let us first be aware of the common misinterpretations of Talent we find in everyday life.

Misinterpretations of Talent

1. *The limited arena of Talent*

The use of the term 'Talent' is common in the art or entertainment world. Some people tend to have a subconscious misinterpretation that Talent only refers to creative ability. This might be deeply rooted in our early years. For example, I remember how my elementary school teacher would address my friend, who was great at singing, as 'talented' and another student, who was great at solving math problems, as 'smart'. Whereas it could have actually been said that one person had musical intelligence while the other was talented in being logical.

For some years in my past organizational role, I was intensely involved in the talent management department. When I mentioned my role to acquaintances, for some strange reason they always assumed I worked in a talent agency looking for new rising stars or celebrities. While I didn't do any auditions to find soap opera actors, I did run selection processes to find the right type of people the organization needed. Nevertheless, I always felt a little awkward explaining we didn't cast anyone to star in a movie.

The conversation would continue with my describing how companies usually have a talent management department—or, as some prefer to call it, a Human Resources department—and how my role included selection processes, leadership development programs, and performance appraisals. Now I think about it, these people's wrong assumptions could have been affected by the exponential growth of 'instant-celeb' reality shows on television.

2. *Assessing Talent based on result or achievement*

While there are people who think they have zero Talent, a lot of others are unsure about their ultimate Talent, for they are capable of doing many different things and produce decent—even great—results in various areas. It may seem they have too many Talents, and are then acknowledged by society as 'multi-talented'. The title is reassuring and encouraging for many people, but it can create confusion for others. People may feel unsure whether they really have a natural Talent for everything they do well, or whether they simply possess the endurance to work hard and achieve their goals.

Society commonly sees Talent as related to a person's ability to perform a particular activity producing an above-average result compared to their peers in the same field. Talent is also used as a subject of competition in reality shows. However, in the *real* reality, although Talent *can* be observed, it should not be assessed via results and—more importantly—it should never be compared.

Talent does play an important role in the process, but is definitely not an ultimate factor, determining the quality of a result. A result can be produced through hard work, continuous practice, luck, and other variables. A great result can be achieved even when a person doesn't have the relevant Talent. On the other hand, it is also possible for someone who is very talented at something to still be incapable of delivering decent results. Achievement is not a reflection of Talent.

3. *Generalization of Talent development in practice*

A lot of companies use the term 'talent management' in addressing a department, or function, whose main role is to develop the skills and knowledge of their employees. While some of them know exactly how to convert that role into correct practice, there are others who approach it as if conducting a chemistry class for high school students.

One huge misunderstanding of Talent development in practice, is when all employees are 'forced' to learn certain skills and knowledge in exactly the same way, and are expected to produce precisely the same result. The misjudgment of an employee's quality due to a false role allocation is definitely not rare. For every individual, talent is unique and closely related to one's personality. It cannot be generalized. Talent allocation, development, and assessment in an organization should not be practiced using a general approach. The key to enable the success of a high performance team, is to acknowledge and appreciate the differences of each person's Talent, then approach each of them differently.

4. *Is it Talent? Or, Passion?*

Another misconception about Talent comes from the trends and hypes in society regarding the notion of 'just following your Passion'. A lot of people say that, in order for us to discover our Talent, we should recall the activities we are so thrilled to do that we feel like we're losing track of time when we do them. When people have the courage to separate the manifestations of Talent and Passion, they will understand there is always the possibility of liking something greatly, while not having the particular Talent needed to excel in that ability.

For example, while watching a singing competition on television, you hear one contestant who sings passionately from their heart. As an audience—as an amateur in music—you can actually notice their voice is steadily out of pitch. Though it is true the singer has a Passion for singing, there's a possibility they are not talented in sensing the accurate notes they intend to produce with their voices.

Most of the time this is innate and can't be developed in the way you might learn a vocal technique. While it is easy for us to hear the incongruity, it might be quite difficult for the singer to realize it, since they have been passionate about singing all their life. Therefore, although Talent should never be compared, external observation is needed to *recognize* a Talent. It is different from how we discover Passion through the internal exploration of what we yearn to do.

"Okay we hear you, Talent can be confusing. So what exactly is Talent?"

Talent is natural. It is innate. It originates in our DNA and is partly affected by the environment where we are raised in our early years. Do you remember that friend who talks about common things but is somehow always amusing by nature? There are those who learn, and try to remember, the best joke in the world but don't sound natural when delivering it. If they didn't have the Talent, they would not even feel as comfortable as a person who is talented at being funny might.

We can recognize Talent through the patterns of spontaneous behaviors, feelings, or thoughts in certain circumstances. In a simple definition, Talent can be understood as a natural aptitude or natural potential. It is an asset, or personal capital, to be accomplished in certain skills. Talent is an inborn gift.

> *"Talent reflects how you're hard-wired. That's what sets the concept apart from that of knowledge or skills. Talent dictates your moment-by-moment reactions to your environment - there's an instinctiveness, an immediacy implied."*
> Kathie Sorensen and Steve Crabtree, 2000

When we talk about practicality, I'm a true believer that any knowledge can be learned and skills developed through hard work and practice. Having, or not having, any particular Talent is not the ultimate factor for success, but having a particular Talent would make the learning process faster. It also gives an authentic signature to a skill.

Talent plays a crucial role in how efficient it is for a person to learn something and how natural it is for them to react, respond, or feel in a certain way. While listening is a practical skill that anyone can train and develop, a sense of empathy is innate. A consultant or facilitator might feel that it is only natural to get a better understanding of another's emotion, and yet have no clue how they achieve it. They are on autopilot. When other people feel that doing something is a challenge, but we feel it is automatic, there is a huge possibility it is our Talent.

Having a particular Talent, however, doesn't necessarily make one better than others. A tangible result and quality are not solely driven by Talent. We can say that one tennis player has more well-developed skills compared to his opponent, but we can never say that he is more talented than the other. As we discussed earlier, Talent cannot be compared, but it can make *your* ability stand out from others. It does not make you better, but it makes you *different*.

Talent delivers our skills in a special way. Talent is unique. It always has a close connection with our personality. One's Talent can be different from that of others, even though it may manifest in the same activities. When you see amazing photographers, some might have the Talent to see from a different perspective, but they might also have a Talent in telling stories through a picture, or have the Talent to capture the right moment. When you see someone who is great in sales, they can be talented in being persuasive, but they can also be talented in being empathic to what their client feels and needs.

As external observers, we can say someone is good at doing something, but the actor is the only one able to say what it is about it that makes it natural for them to do. Anyone can learn various public speaking techniques, but any great public speaker is significantly different from others. One might produce a powerful speech through a deep voice, or their intonation, or body language, while another is compelling through their ability to connect with an audience. Yet another is well-known for their ability to amuse and entertain.

All of them are great through their own 'signatures', and they are authentic. They know what their natural Talent is, and they know how it plays a crucial role in making them special. That is how you excel in certain skills: through being authentic, and using your Talent.

Talent is inborn. It is God's gift, no matter what your spiritual belief is. You may feel it in circumstances where you feel you can do something naturally without too much difficulty, as if your senses were created and destined to do so.

I strongly believe there must be a reason why you are given such potential. Since it is a 'potential', it might not yet be visible or unleashed. While it is understood to be a gift that everyone has, it's sometimes quite difficult to be aware of what our natural Talent is.

Unfortunately, due to particular circumstances, Talent is often neglected or, even worse, forgotten.

How Can It Be Forgotten?

I remember a story my former leader once shared. One of his closest friends—let's call him Bobby—won a singing competition when he was in elementary school. Bobby had always loved singing. Clearly, he had a Talent in music that was easy for the public to recognize. He was happy and thrilled when he got his trophy. A few days later, Bobby's mother came to his school and met with the school principal.

During this sudden meeting, Bobby's mother was furious and asked the school to not include Bobby in singing competitions anymore. Bobby's mother thought that such competitions would interfere with Bobby's academic study and give Bobby the idea he could get away with not excelling in other, 'normal', subjects.

Most of us were raised in a society that thinks the world is one giant competition, and that we need to win this one game if we don't want to be seen as a failure. Our education system—at least in the culture I've been raised in—has been training our minds in this way since forever.

We are wired to perceive that some subjects in school are more important than others. We are also instilled with the perception that a brilliant student is the one who can get good grades in all academic subjects. Well-rounded achievements are valued greatly, driven by the fear of losing this 'competition' called life, while a Talent not perceived as useful for general academic subjects is underrated.

It is often ignored how Talent is unique and special to every person. Sometimes we forget how Talent should be appreciated as an inborn gift and how all of us should have the privilege to develop it to lead a much more fulfilling life.

When we are young it is easy to be encouraged, or discouraged, about something, especially when the Talent we naturally have is not considered to be prestigious in our social framework. It seems like a lot of children are educated according to a fear of the future rather than out of respect for their freedom to express, explore, and develop their natural Talent. This might be one of the most fundamental reasons why most of people are not aware of their Talent.

"...and my contention is, all kids have tremendous talents. And we squander them, pretty ruthlessly.
So, I want to talk about education and I want to talk about creativity.
My contention is that creativity now is as
important in education as literacy, and we should treat it with the same status."
-Sir Ken Robinson

Unfortunately, this condition doesn't get much better once we reach adulthood. There's nothing wrong in learning and developing necessary skills. Some practical skills will always come in handy, anyway. Yet, according to Kathie Sorensen and Steve Crabtree from Gallup, there's a chance that, while we are putting our time and efforts into areas of non-Talent, we're leaving our true Talent unrevealed. This may lead to circumstances where people are stuck in mediocrity.

Such a condition keeps occurring in a lot of workplaces. Some companies only base their core assessments on competencies. They also try to develop particular skills that lead to direct results, merely through general methods. Some organizations neglect the fact that people have different personalities—Talent differences—and different ways of learning and performing at their best.

A person who has Talent in being persuasive might find it easy to learn sales and marketing. While someone who is highly innovative and has a Talent in ideation might find it challenging to transfer their innovative ideas into a concrete action plan. They might need to collaborate with a practical person in the team.

When a person values responsibility and they are committed to deliver a result, they would be able to perform regardless of having a suitable Talent. But, in the long run, it might have a negative impact on them, and even on the organization. Without the space to channel their authentic Talent, an employee might feel uninspired, stuck, bored, or even frustrated. A person who has a Talent to be empathic might be able to do some accounting once in a while, but they would be burned out if they only interacted with numbers every single day. Therefore, a right role allocation and a tailored development program are crucial for an organization in handling their employees.

When we understand human beings possess their own unique, inborn and natural, aptitudes, we will be able to finally explore, and focus our effort toward combining what we love doing with what we are naturally good at.

Unwrapping the Inborn Gift in 3 Simple Steps

While skills are commonly more visible, and easier to recognize, based on results, Talent is considered to be more discreet. It is more personal and sometimes uneasy to describe. It gets even harder if a person has been trapped in an environment that makes them forget their natural aptitude. In order to start rediscovering our Talent, it requires honesty and an effort to explore our true self.

1. Explore, explore, explore

It took some time for me to start this chapter. The most challenging part was actually to connect with my own experience in discovering my Talent. As far as I remember, making a serious effort to openly explore your Talent was really not a hot topic in the environment where I grew up. It was definitely nothing in comparison to having academic achievements.

Internally, I remembered I always felt uneasy declaring I had a certain Talent. I felt it would be considered arrogant to claim I was naturally good at something. There were also those 'what if' thoughts: What if I was actually mediocre in that area? What if I tried one thing, and I wasn't as good as others at doing it? What if my Talent was not important? Then I realized that, in understanding my Talent, my mind was my own worst enemy.

One way I accidentally discovered a great method to start unwrapping my Talent was when I moved out from my hometown to university and started an independent life. This opportunity allowed me to see my life as an empty canvas. I tried out a lot of different things, including martial arts, first aid training, traditional dances, event management, and different kinds of student organizations. I learned the beauty of exploration and the art of accepting challenges. I learned to let go of my ego and my desire to always be great and, instead, I had fun enjoying of a lot of different new worlds.

And, much later, I realized that one of these worlds led to the discovery of an 'unknown' within me. It was not unwrapped in one particular moment; it was more a process of slowly peeling away my old beliefs and fear in order to discover one true core.

After being actively involved in the global youth organization and interacting with countless different people from many backgrounds and cultures, I realized I had an aptitude for being empathic. It is just natural for me to feel connected to, and to understand, other people's emotions, especially those whom I directly interact with.

Sometimes it could feel overwhelming to absorb the intensity of everybody's emotions in one room and it would drain my energy to function properly. I realized every Talent has a downside: it could become harmful. But, with the right level of management, this Talent of empathy helps me understand a person's condition. It helps me make certain important decisions and facilitate other people in understanding themselves.

By now, you may have had this thought: "But I don't have that much time to explore anymore. I have my full time job and I have other responsibilities." Your concern is absolutely normal. At the end of this chapter you will discover how to explore within the time and space you currently have.

2. Take external voices as clues in the search for your treasure

During the process of writing this book, I got to talk to some of my friends who I consider have an awareness of their Talent. Rudy (not his real name) is one of those people who understands who he is and is really comfortable in being himself. I once asked him—out of all the skills and abilities he has—what his natural Talent was and how he came to know about it. He answered firmly that his Talent was 'being funny'.

He felt it was just natural for him to think of and create jokes in his head, then wait for the right time to tell them. This would happen in just the blink of an eye. He also mentioned how his relatives, friends, and acquaintances laugh at his jokes. They also laugh at the things he does, and some of his relatives even laugh when he doesn't do anything. They said they laugh because of his radiant, comical face.

I asked him when he first realized he had this Talent. Apparently, Rudy was a really quiet kid. He only told jokes to his close friends because he always wanted to play safe. But this was only up to his time in junior high school, when his friend told him something that convinced him otherwise: "You are actually funny!"

If he hadn't listened to his friend in school, and if he wasn't aware of his relatives' fondness of his jokes, Rudy would never have known he is talented at being funny. He would not have understood he had this gift for naturally sharing joy and happiness with other people.

This Talent, nurtured by Rudy's endless hard work in networking and learning, has brought him to different kinds of professional experiences in local and international corporations. This was how he realized he has a Passion for human resource management and development. Now—in his early 30s—he is considering exploring the entertainment world, where he can bring positivity not only to his family and colleagues, but to larger groups of people as well.

From Rudy's story, we can see how showcasing our ability, and seeing how people evaluate our potential, can give us a clue to our Talent. Sometimes, those people who are close to us can see something beyond what we see ourselves. Such objective, external assessment can be done not only in an official way—for example, by a series of psychology tests—but also through small discussions. These clues exist in the simple interactions and assessments that arise casually, such as:

"You have a way with words."

"There is something empowering about the way you speak."

"Your drawing moves me."

"The way you analyze a case is impressive: you can see what others can't."

"I don't know what it is, but I just feel positive around you."

"Your voice soothes me."

"It's amazing how you can always connect with any kind of person."

"You are actually funny!"

To some extent, this type of assessment can be a good clue in getting closer to understanding our natural aptitude: our Talent. However, accepting all kinds of assessments without a good filter could lead us into confusion, insecurity, and fear. We need to remember that the main objective in listening attentively to external assessment is *only* to explore our possible Talent. In this discovery stage, we should only listen to the positive auto-responses people give about what we do. Any negative external assessment, or feedback, will help us in the later process of our self-growth and development. Moreover, the exploration would work in a complete cycle of discovery *only* if we added an internal validation: the voice that comes from within one's self.

3. What is it that I'm naturally good at?

Other people can give you assessments. They can praise you for how great you are, for the things you do, or for something you create with your bare hands. However, while the net result of your restless nights, effort, and hard work to achieve greatness might indicate Talent to other people, you actually may not feel it has been *natural* for you to have worked in this way. Therefore, another process crucial to unwrapping your inborn gift is to turn on the validation mode within yourself.

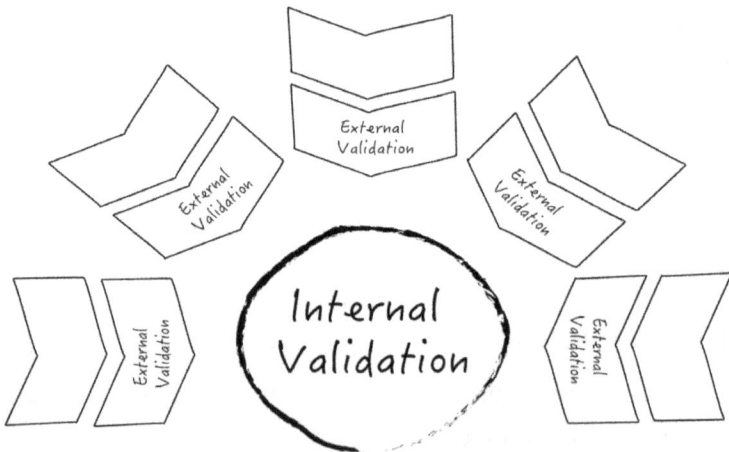

While receiving input from external sources, our inner self will give a response in order to validate whether the statement was accurate to some extent. Your inner voice will tell you exactly what it is you're naturally good at. Only we, ourselves, can discover the core strength that drives our ability. But, what was planted in us that makes our creations good?

Anyone can be good at writing and develop their writing skills through lots of practice, but J.K. Rowling and Mark Manson have a specific Talent. We can taste it in their writing. What is it that feels natural for you in creating a good result? Is it your imaginative nature? Is it your aptitude for being logical in producing a good flow? Is it the way you express yourself in words? Is it your creativity? Or, is it your ability to reflect?

When your team-mates tell you that you are a good leader, there might be tons of attributes of a great leader. What exactly is it that stands out? Which part of it feels natural to you, that you just do automatically? Is it being strategic in solving problems? Is it being supportive and practical? Is it being adaptive? Or, is it being visionary? Certainly, a person can have multiple Talents.

Find the core strength that gives your creation an authentic taste. You might have been ignoring it because it seems just like any other thing you do. It feels natural for you. It feels too normal, and not special. But that's exactly why it is, indeed, special. Not everyone has it, and you have it *within* you.

Talent is ONLY a Seed

In discovering your Purpose, Talent plays an important role as capital: as an asset loaned to you by the Creator. It needs to be used, managed, and developed so you can play your role during the period of your lifetime. It is, indeed, an inborn gift. However, discovering your natural Talent will not lead you straight away to the top. Unused Talent can be a waste. A mismanaged Talent could even bring harm.

Talent is a resource for your future journey. Yet, it is only a seed and definitely not a tree. In order to grow a fruitful tree, a lot of effort needs to be made. There are a lot of factors to consider and ingredients to be added. If you have ever tried to grow a plant from seed, you would know that to get a healthy plant, and harvest great fruit, you need a strong commitment to continually take care of it. You also need to have high quality soil and the right type of temperatures.

In order for us to be skillful, we need continuous effort, much learning, good practices, and hard work. Talent will give us the right push during the process. Moreover, if we want to reach a level of mastery, we will need an endless process of learning. 'Endless' means it can literally take forever. There will be ongoing exploration—continual trial and error. A painter never puts down his brush and says "I'm already too good at this". A legendary singer never stops practicing their singing feeling they have beautifully mastered any kind of song. The more a person becomes skillful in one area—especially when they also love what they do—the more they would want to learn and improve. They always want to explore, and climb to, the unknown limit of their potential.

For practical purposes, we will not talk here about mastering only one skill. When we talk about managing and developing a Talent to be used in a purposeful career journey, we do not need to wait until we feel we are the expert in a particular skill. Living a career is also a learning journey. Along the way, we continually improve our skills and qualities: it will always be a learn-by-doing process.

A skill will start to be beneficial for a career when it reaches a decent level after some period of training in a safe environment. It's like when you learn how to dive: you would start by learning some basic skills in a swimming pool until you reach some level of readiness, then you will go into the deep blue sea.

One way to measure whether a Talent has been utilized, managed, and developed to a decent level of skill is when it starts to have a business value: there is someone willing to give away, or sacrifice, something they have to purchase your service or product. As we found in discussing the previous topic, it is a common belief that any skill can be developed to a decent level, even if one doesn't have the natural Talent to achieve this. On the other hand, Talent without practice and hard work would be left worthless and give us nothing but an unplanted seed. Therefore, discovering Talent is one small first step—the stubbornness and perseverance in utilizing, managing, and growing it are what makes a difference.

Discover Your Talent

Now that we understand how every single one of us has had the gifts since we were born, I would like to invite you to communicate with your inner self to unwrap your Talent.

Estimated duration: 60 minutes

Give yourself time to focus completely on yourself,
without any distraction. Remember you are allowed to answer the
questions in any method possible
(e.g. simple writing, drawing, painting, cutting/attaching pictures,
mind-mapping etc.)

1. If you have any brief ideas on what you're good at, try to list them all.

2. If you are still unsure, it is suggested you allocate some time to explore different kinds of things.

You might already be occupied with your daily routines and activities, but that doesn't mean you can't spare time to understand yourself even better.

a. *Keeping your own time schedule in mind, try to list five different things you might want to try this month. (You may repeat each activity 3-5 times)*

b. *Also, try to schedule a feasible time when you might do these things.*

c. *Try to observe and journal what you feel throughout the process of exploring these new types of activities. Was there anything that felt natural for you to do?*

After answering question no. 1 or 2, please choose a few people (minimum three) who you trust have a credible and objective assessment and opinion of you, or the particular activities you do. Have a conversation with them in order to understand their honest evaluation of the activities you've done, or the results you've created. You can refer to the following questions as a guide:

Generally, what do they think you are good at?

Note down their statements and pay attention to the way they phrase them

What do they think of the quality of the particular
activities you did?

_____

_____

_____

_____

What was good about it? What made it
different or special?

_____

_____

_____

_____

What do they think about any potential,
or Talent, you may have?

_____

_____

_____

_____

_____

Now, after this conversation with other people, it's time for you to do an internal validation. Out of the statements and assessments on what you are good at, ask yourself which ones sound right for you? Do you feel like you're actually good at something others tell you? What's in it that sounds relevant? What's the source of it? What's in you that makes you able to do it? What feels natural for you in doing it? You probably don't put much effort into doing it, or you do it without trying, so what's in it that becomes your automatic response in almost all similar conditions? What is you core strength?

For example, when you say you are good at doing a presentation, what do you think you are good at? Is it the process of visualizing data in graphs and pictures? Is it being logical? Is it being detail oriented? Is it how you can connect with an audience? Is it being creative? Is it being strategic? Is it being persuasive?

To help you understand more about why these things feel natural for you, look back at the 1st **Special Page,** where you explored your personality type, specifically your strengths. Does why it feels natural for you to do these things, make more sense now?

Feel free to write down all of your possible Talents,

then try to prioritize as many as five natural aptitudes you feel are strongly relevant to you.

1. _____

2. _____

3. _____

4. _____

5. _____

After deciding your top five Talents, elaborate why you think you have Talent in these areas. You can try to describe some other concrete activities you may not have already mentioned, but which you have experienced in the past, where you also showed these Talents.

I have Talent in   Because

1.

2.

3.

4.

5.

Journaling

Congratulations on finishing the set of activities in the chapter 'A Seed Called Talent'! I hope you enjoyed the process.

Now, please spare around 15 minutes to do a little journaling. You may respond to this question in any method you like.

How was your journey in discovering your Talent?

How do you feel about the process so far?

What are the new realizations or reconfirmations that you got from this chapter?

Is there anything new you just realized about yourself?

How do you see the connection between the result of your Passions and Talents? How do you think your Talents can help you to excel in your skills and give a signature to your ability?

Do you still have any unanswered questions?

"When I made Facebook two years ago my goal was to help people understand what was going on in their world a little better. I wanted to create an environment where people could share whatever information they wanted, but also have control over whom they shared that information with. I think a lot of the success we've seen is because of these basic principles... It's not because of the amount of money. For me and my colleagues, the most important thing is that we create an open information flow for people. Having media corporations owned by conglomerates is just not an attractive idea to me... The thing I really care about is the mission, making the world open."

Mark Zuckerberg (open letter, 2006)

Chapter 7

Contribution - the One that Gives Meaning

Not everyone is aware of the primary mission, and the main reason, why Facebook was created in the first place. In fact, not many people have a clear idea what was in the minds of some of our world changers and global movers when they decided to build something: something that would eventually become giant businesses or brilliant products. People may know how fat their bank accounts are, or the value of their cars, but these factors are apparently not at all why they originally chose to start such a difficult yet fulfilling journey: one that happens to shape our world today.

The most brilliant ideas usually come from a desire to provide a solution to a problem. That desire reflects a human need to find and possess meaning. It is a desire that comes from our deepest heart. This is exactly what we want to explore further: the desire to make a Contribution.

There's a reason why this element is being revealed as the final stage in discovering one's Purpose. Passion gives us joy, while Talent is the capital to achieve greatness. The combination of Passion and Talent already brings us closer to our goals and achievements in life. However, lots of highly influential people are driven to work extremely hard at more than just what they love doing, and what they're good at. Their solid determination is driven by a clarity of reason. It is motivated by a clarity of Contribution: the one element that gives a strong sense of meaning. Contribution can be understood as something we do for others in order to see an improvement in their condition. Hence, Contribution can only be revealed through an intense

"To organize the world's information and make it universally accessible and useful."

Google

"To make a contribution to the world by making tools for the mind that advance humankind."

Steve Jobs' mission statement for Apple in 1980

"The inventor... looks upon the world and is not content with things as they are. He wants to improve whatever he sees, he wants to benefit the world; he is haunted by an idea."

Alexander Graham Bell

"One day you will wake up and there won't be any more time to do things you've always wanted. Do it now." "The world is in the hands of those who have the courage to DREAM and to realize their dreams. "

Paulo Coelho

"To passionately campaign for the protection of the environment, human and civil rights, and against animal testing within the cosmetics and toiletries industries."

Body Shop - Britain

"To create a better every-day life for the people we aim to serve."

IKEA – Mission Statement

interaction with the world, and to explore it will take another level of openness, honesty, and courage.

The process of understanding the element of Contribution doesn't necessarily need to be as rigidly ordered as the final stage of discovering Purpose. It is, however, a little bit more challenging, because this is the part where we need to have the humility to see the world as it is. It is the part where we need to understand how the world has countless problems and needs our help. It doesn't mean you need to build the next Google. It doesn't mean you need to build the next huge thing in the world. It doesn't even mean you need to start a business. It could start from a very simple thing you might do for the improvement of your own surroundings: the improvement of one condition that matters to your heart.

"Have you ever thought that understanding what you love doing and understanding your inborn gift might be a clue to something bigger? We only have a short amount of time to live on earth, What would be a role that is trusted and given to us in this short time?"

The Clarity of Why

The journey to fulfilling Purpose is always far from easy. Devoting yourself to providing a solution and improving one's condition will be a long and winding road, unsafe and sometimes illogical. Not everyone will be able to see what you envision. The fact you're reading this paragraph at the moment might be the stage when you need to see the options and decide whether to go on the safe path or take the road less traveled.

If the road of Contribution is difficult and unsafe, then why are there individuals who still want to strive for this road less traveled?

Apart from the external driver—the fact that our world has countless problems, giving us tons of different solutions to contribute—there is also another reason that comes from the inside. To understand this internal driver, we need to expand the discussion of understanding human motivation. One popular theory on this topic was formulated by Abraham Maslow.

Maslow's theory of the hierarchy of needs captured different levels of human motivation, with the idea that human beings are driven to act by different factors, according to their needs. This theory is often pictured in the shape of a pyramid with the most basic needs at its base and the need for self-actualization at the top.

The first four basic layers of the pyramid show 'deficiency needs'—esteem, friendship and love, security, and physical requirements—while the motivation of people who go beyond the scope of basic needs and strive for continual improvement is known as 'meta-motivation': the satisfaction of 'growth needs'.

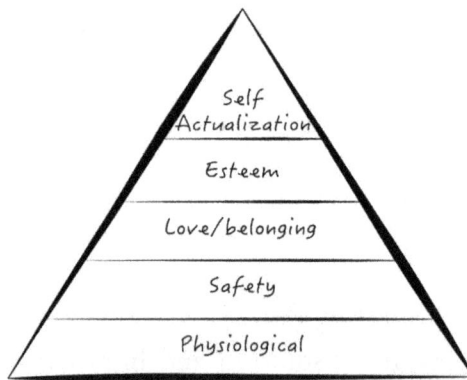

The level of self-actualization—which can be defined as 'the desire to accomplish everything that one can, or to become the best possible version of ourselves'—reflects the fact that, as they mature, human beings become more aware of their *selfhood* and are driven even more by a sense of personal meaning.

In further studies, Maslow's later thoughts improved his original theory beyond the implication self-actualization was the highest need, and the final step in the hierarchy. He noticed that human beings tend to continually seek extraordinary experiences, which he termed 'peak experiences'. These are the type of special experiences that produce a strong sensation, such as bliss, or are considered profound, and provide a better understanding of one's self.

Therefore, Maslow added an extra level of motivation beyond self-actualization. He called it 'self-transcendence'. Self-transcendence is described as the desire to transcend, or go beyond one's ego, or even beyond human consciousness. Maslow further elaborated that, when a person is undergoing these peak experiences, they are able to separate from themselves. In this way, they feel like they belong to something bigger than themselves—they feel more united with the world. The process of reaching such a state of bliss and experiencing higher meaning may involve service to others, or supporting a cause by giving a Contribution according to their potential.

HIERARCHY OF NEED
ST = Self-Transcedence

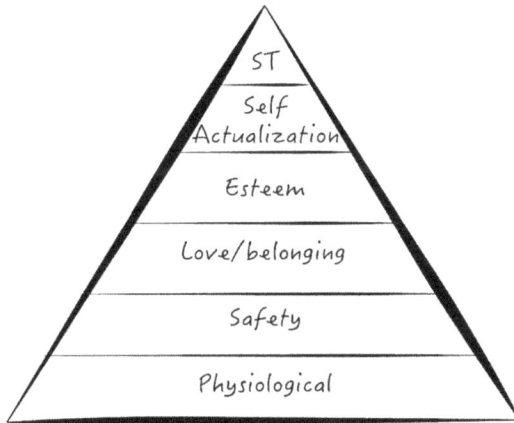

Reflecting on this later development of Maslow's theory, we can see how it is in our nature to serve others and that we desire to contribute something good toward others. Human beings feel positive and experience joy and deeper meaning when they see other people are happy, especially when they know they have contributed toward creating that happiness.

There has been varied psychological research into the connection between happiness and kindness. One study, conducted by Allan Luks, marked the introduction of the term 'Helper's High'. Helper's High can be described as the powerful feeling—the pleasurable, and euphoric, emotional sensation—people experience when they help others. In a survey of thousands of volunteers in the United States, Luks found there were constant positive reports from people who had helped others, stating that their health status had been improving. Many of them said the improvement started showing up after they began their volunteer activities. Half of the participants reported they experienced a high feeling, 43 percent felt energetic and stronger, 23 percent experienced a warm sensation, 22 percent felt more relaxed and calmer, 21 percent admitted to having greater feelings of self-worth, and 13 percent experienced fewer aches and pains.

Fundamentally, rather than being a self-righteous act, giving a Contribution actually can be considered a selfless act with a selfish reason. We don't contribute because we feel superior and think others are wrong, or in a lower state than us. When we do good and contribute goodness to other people, we experience pure happiness and a positive sensation.

Imagine if we understood it as our life's mission: if we are able to do it in our lifetime and see the result of positive change. It is the idea of altruism—we have done good to others and made our Contribution toward making someone else's condition better—that makes us feel good about ourselves. It gives core meaning to our everyday life. Contribution is the essence of Purpose. This is the final puzzle in understanding the reason for your existence: the key answer to how you can play a role in creating a certain impact. Your 'significant role' may not change a whole generation, or create a massive global transformation (or it may—who knows?), but by what you do with your hands, you could make the world slightly better—and do you know how great that would feel?

But, Seriously, Why?

If giving Contribution is so fulfilling, why do people tend to be unaware of this fact? Why does it seem like this recipe for happiness is unknown? The fact it is human nature for people to feel happy when they contribute to helping those in need is not the world's best-kept secret. Deep down inside, we all know it. Even little kids know it. Have you ever witnessed a three-year-old clean a table without anyone asking them to, or a four-year-old giving a hug to their crying friend? We think they are so cute for doing it. Well, actually, they don't act cute. They just act that way because it naturally feels good for them. What is the problem with adults? Why do some people tend to forget their calling to contribute to others?

Here's one potential reason. When we reach adulthood, for different reasons and different experiences, it is just easy for us to feel we are not good enough—we are not mature enough, we are not smart enough, we are not rich enough. This can be the result of a compilation of past experiences, trauma, old beliefs, or social pressure. It is common to feel scared of not being 'enough', and therefore not being accepted in the society we want to belong to. Though it is usually left unsaid, it is deeply rooted in our adult heart.

When we don't feel 'enough', it becomes quite an issue to think we have the capacity to make Contribution. We might feel we don't even have enough for ourselves, therefore we cannot give anything to others. Some people start to feel *"It's probably better to think about myself first, to feel I have enough and am secure, and then I will contribute"*. In this kind of condition, questioning 'when' would promote a vicious cycle.

As we grow older, we do indeed have more needs and responsibilities. We do eventually face circumstances where we need to be the provider not only for ourselves, but for our family and relatives. While it is inevitable to see financial variables as core factors in securing basic needs, we sometimes fail to distinguish between what we primarily *need* and what we simply desire to *have*. And, we then mistake that second factor as being an important element in making us feel 'enough'.

Our needs and lifestyle go along with our capacity to earn. We did not have the need to go to a certain coffee shop when we were in elementary school but, now we have the capacity to buy a cup of branded coffee, the atmosphere of a particular coffee shop may become important, even necessary, for some of us to simply function.

Our needs grow bigger, our standard of comfort and safety shift. Viral advertisements and appealing commercial marketing strategies also do not help much. It is messages like 'You would look better if you use this. You would feel great when you do that. You would feel more comfortable if you buy this', that strengthen the belief that we are not 'enough'. They subconsciously increase an adult's fear and promote misleading solutions for our self-esteem since it is one of a human being's basic needs to be accepted in society. Thus, we always feel the need to have more things, and it is endless.

It is well within anyone's right to choose a particular lifestyle, as long as it doesn't harm others. The core reason in understanding this condition in our society—the continual impact of daily marketing messages— is not to say it is wrong to choose a particular brand or to want some high quality product or service. When people have the capacity to purchase, and the ability to choose, among different options there's nothing wrong about having some specific preference for themselves. The importance of having this discussion is to realize there is a common tendency in our society for people to pursue materials beyond their capacity to do so, in order to impress others. Some purchases are subconsciously driven out of fear; for example, when customers buy in order for them to feel better about themselves, and to feel they can be accepted and perceived as 'ideal' by their surroundings.

Without a clear understanding of the core reason, this overbuying tendency will never reach an end. This type of conversation is crucial to remind us how impossible it is for human beings to feel completely secure in satisfying the ongoing demands of our 'noisy' world. It is to see we will never be able to fully catch up with what we think society expects us to be.

Sometimes, it is not about the reality of one extreme or another: whether we are completely secure or we are experiencing scarcity. It is not about not having bread when we are physically starving—it can be a feeling of craving when our stomach is actually full. It can be something that is deeply rooted but unseen: when the feeling of 'not enough' is sourced from the emptiness of one's soul. The process of making ourselves feel good enough—continually following external demands— can actually make us feel even emptier inside.

This is the unfortunate truth: eventually there is a really slim chance for a person to ever arrive at that stage of "*I feel completely 'enough' and safe. This is the time for me to contribute*". Financial concerns usually become the common reason people give to delay or neglect their natural desire to contribute. If that were the case, there would never be an ultimate, perfect moment to start contributing. While it is not realistic to say that money should not be a factor in making decisions, our ability to Contribute versus our financial viability should not necessarily be an issue.

When we listen to our human desire to give Contribution, we shouldn't see it as an act of withdrawing what we have so we will have less than before. It is actually *sharing* what has been given to us and possibly receiving even more in return, though in a different shape or form.

Moreover, Contribution should not be perceived as an obstacle to financial gain and stability. It doesn't necessarily need to be delivered through an extreme act of sacrifice and suffering. We can indeed make a living by contributing, and there's nothing wrong with that. There are limitless ways to have a career that can contribute great things to society, such as being an independent professional, or having various roles in corporate sectors that have a vision to improve the state of society.

Contribution can be—and, I think, *should* be—delivered in a balanced way. Trust that when you do good, you will always be provided for, and will believe that you are 'enough'.

Everyone has their own time to arrive at the moment when they need to seek the calling to contribute. Some people don't even have the privilege to start questioning, nor have the courage to strive to find it, until their final day. But, they who have any anxiety or questions regarding in what way, and how, they can give meaning to their lives, eventually need a serious level of humility to learn what it is about the world that breaks their hearts. They also need to be honest about wanting to take part in providing a solution. They need clarity of mind—and creativity—to find the right way to contribute in a balanced way. In many cases, they will need the courage to take an adventure in order to understand it. And it needs an even greater courage to answer the call.

"And now here is my secret,
a very simple secret: It is only with the heart that one can see rightly;
what is essential is invisible to the eye."

Antoine de Saint-Exupéry (The Little Prince, 1943)

My Adventure, My Reminder

It was September 2014. I decided to go on an adventure to find an answer to a question I was not even sure about. I had already known I wanted to do something in life for a greater meaning, but was doubtful whether I was ready to take the life-long commitment of choosing 'the road less traveled'. I also did not know how I would concretely do so. So, there I was. I had decided to take on a short-term volunteer project.

I was assigned to work in a children's foundation in the Philippines for a six-week period. It was in a rather small, but homely, shelter. There were around ten babies in one room (males and females), and fourteen older girls in another room. The ages of the babies ranged from zero to three, while the girls varied from four up to around sixteen years. Not only did I get to interact with, and take care of, some of the most beautiful children in the world, I also got pretty close to the carers, who I called 'Ate', which means older sister in Tagalog. From them, I learnt almost all the background stories of the kids.

There was a four-year-old girl, let's call her Melissa, who was quite reserved. Little did I know that Melissa was apparently 'rescued' some years previously (when she was less than a year old) with cigarette burns on her head. It was also discovered her mother's boyfriend had raped her. No doubt it would have affected her psychological condition.

Another baby I fell in love with was named Dannie (not her real name). She was two years old when I first met her. She was beyond adorable. She always raised both her arms up high whenever she met a visitor, asking to be carried and hugged. One caretaker told me Dannie's biological father was a tricycle driver. Tricycles are one of the public transportation systems in the Philippines. She was brought to the children's foundation because she was the eleventh child in the family and they didn't have adequate finances to even feed her.

These are only two out of the ten stories of the babies I got the privilege to take care of during the project. My job description was simple: to share affection and love with them while helping them do basic activities. Taking care of the babies gave me indescribable warmth. It built an emotional connection that was—and still is—very close to my heart. It felt like it was not me who gave *them* love, but that I was actually the receiver. In the first couple of weeks, apart from the strong affection we shared, I wasn't able to connect the dots as to how this volunteering experience could give me clues about how to contribute in life. Then, came a time when I arrived at a strong revelation. The pieces of the puzzle finally fell into place.

On the third week of the project, I got the chance to work with the older girls in the shelter. I gave tutorials every afternoon after they arrived back from school. I sometimes also gave them some fun sessions: we sang, we danced, and we also learned interesting facts about different countries.

It was actually a little bit more challenging to interact with the older girls, since it took time for them to warm up and be open with strangers. But, once they trusted me, I had a blast sharing knowledge and joy with them every single day. As I got closer to them, I started to realize something. I noticed that these kids developed more slowly than most other children raised by their parents. There was an eleven-year-old girl who was in the second year of primary school and she still had difficulties reading. There was also a three-year-old who had not yet started to speak. I couldn't help but imagine that similar circumstances would happen to Melissa, Dannie, and the other babies. I felt an inevitable pain in my heart.

I wasn't really aware of the background stories of the older girls. However, from the stories I had heard about Melissa and Dannie, I had no doubt the reasons why the other kids had arrived in the shelter were not too different. Obviously, none of the children had done anything wrong. Melissa and Dannie didn't commit any sin to be left in the shelter. They had just born into an unfortunate and complicated situation.

All of these sweet kids had potential. They had the right to have bright futures. They just happened to be living in a shelter with another twenty-four kids who they called siblings, and were being looked after by around five to seven carers every day. While it was apparent the babies needed more attention in doing basic activities, it was impossible to replicate the focused assistance and the exclusive care given by parents in the early development stages of a child.

I couldn't help but wonder: what if Dannie couldn't get any opportunity to unleash her potential and improve her life? What if Dannie's life situation and condition later left her with a similar fate as her father's? What if Dannie grew up to have lots of children that she couldn't feed, children who also wouldn't have the opportunity to improve their lives?

I started to see how vicious the cycle was. I realized then that those children should have had the chance to dream and to achieve their dreams, and the chance to play important roles in life. If only they could have the opportunity. True, it might need endless hard work to bring about—and it is a matter of choice—but it also requires one, or more, turning points for an individual to have the revelation of choosing the long journey worth taking.

There I found the answer I was looking for. I finally understood the Contribution I wanted to commit to. I was ready to commit to creating the opportunities for people to understand themselves, to give them the chance to unleash their potential, and understand what they truly want to do in life.

On the very last day of my project, I went to the shelter for one last time. I first went to see the babies. I carried and hugged them one by one and whispered some prayers along with giving small kisses on their foreheads. Then I went to the girls' room. I brought a huge bag full of books, which I had managed to collect from my generous friends in the Philippines. I then had a 'grown up' conversation with the girls, talking about dreams and hard work. I knew they might not understand everything I said, but I knew they could understand how much I cared about them and how much I wished them the best. I hope that even when they grow up, they will remember this. Before I left, some of the kids wrote me letters. I still keep them in my wallet.

Ultimately, I'm not sure I did a lot for the kids. Anything I did might not have had any direct correlation in creating a better future for them. However, throughout this adventure, they were the ones who gave *me* the priceless answer: the clarity of the Contribution I wanted to make. That is my story, the story of how the next clue for my calling was able to slip in by way of the adventure I took. And now it's your turn for your calling to find its way to knock at your door.

Only If You Are Ready

To understand what kind of Contribution your soul wants to give, it requires humility, honesty, and courage. It takes a sense of readiness. If you have ongoing questions on what kind of meaning you should have in your life, or if you feel you have a calling within you to take a role in making the world slightly better, this might be the perfect chance for you.

If you're ready, take the time to prepare yourself for an 'adventure'. For this activity, the easiest principle is to just live in the 'here and now'. You don't need to buy a plane ticket to another country to look for an adventure. It can be as simple as turning off your mobile phone completely and going to a place you have never been before in your city, using transportation you may have never used before.

You can even go somewhere familiar, but you set the condition that will enable you to experience something new. You can schedule your solo time, your 'me' time for only a day, or three days, even one week. Yes, it might be a little bit challenging to allocate that much time during your busy days, but try your best to finish all your work and leave your worries behind so you are completely available for this adventure.

Instruction

1. Schedule your solo adventure. If you already have some ideas on what kind of Contribution you want to make, you can arrange the adventure to align with that. For example, if you want to have Contribution in the area of education, you can volunteer in a project to teach kids. If you have a heart for the environment, you can go on an adventure hiking on a mountain, or diving. Decide how long you want to take the journey for and how many times you want to do it.

2. Listen to your inner self. If you already know where you want to go, and which unfamiliar area you want to explore, you don't need to think about any specific reason for choosing a place. However, the less information you have about the place, the better.

3. Decide all the conditions you want to apply during this adventure. For example, only bring a certain amount of cash and no credit card, no mobile phone, or any communication devices—or put them on flight mode during the whole journey. Engage in conversation with three local people. The objective of applying this condition is to enable the unexpected signs from the universe to appear before you and enable you to be present in the 'here and now'.

4. During your adventure do one, or more, simple nice things to three strangers during each journey. It can be as simple as offering someone a seat on public transport, helping an old lady cross the street, or buying a homeless person lunch. Let your senses guide you regarding what to do to for these people in need. Be aware of how you feel during the process, and be completely honest with yourself.

5. Be curious, like a little child! During your trip and observations, generate questions to ask the people you meet—or to simply question yourself.

Journaling

After taking the 'adventure', please spare around 15 minutes to do a little journaling. You may respond to these questions in any way you like.

What were your general findings from the adventure?

_____

_____

_____

_____

_____

What were the nice things you did to strangers? Why did you do them, and how did it make you feel?

_____

_____

_____

_____

_____

Did you notice what was in your surroundings, and was there one fact that broke your heart?

Why did you care about the fact? Did you feel like you wanted to contribute to make it better?

Is there anything new you just realized about yourself?

Congratulations on finishing your adventure throughout
the chapter 'Contribution - the One That Gives Meaning'.

I hope you enjoyed the process. Please keep all your answers, as
we will need them to explore, and finally discover, your **Purpose**.

"Here's to the crazy ones. The misfits. The rebels.
The troublemakers. The round pegs in the square holes.
The ones who see things differently. They're not fond of rules. And they
have no respect for the status quo. You can quote them, disagree with
them, glorify or vilify them. About the only thing you can't do is ignore
them. Because they change things. They push the human race forward.
And, while some may see them as the crazy ones, we see genius.
Because the people who are crazy enough to think they can change the
world, are the ones who do."

Apple, Inc.

3rd Special Page

The Purpose

This is the most important stage in the journey through this book, as you will finally define what your Purpose is, and how it can be the ultimate driver in your career and life

Estimated duration: 30 minutes

Since you have followed all the activities, by now you already have the answers for each of your elements:

your Passion, Talent, and Contribution.

By arranging all of the pieces, it's now time for you to finally solve the puzzle.

On the template on the next page, place all of your answers in the appropriate space using sticky notes.

Here is an example:

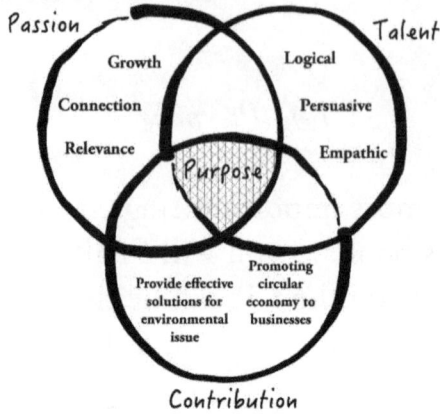

Passion — Growth, Connection, Relevance
Talent — Logical, Persuasive, Empathic
Purpose
Contribution — Provide effective solutions for environmental issue, Promoting circular economy to businesses

"My Purpose is to **catalyze businesses to be sustainable** through **consultation**"

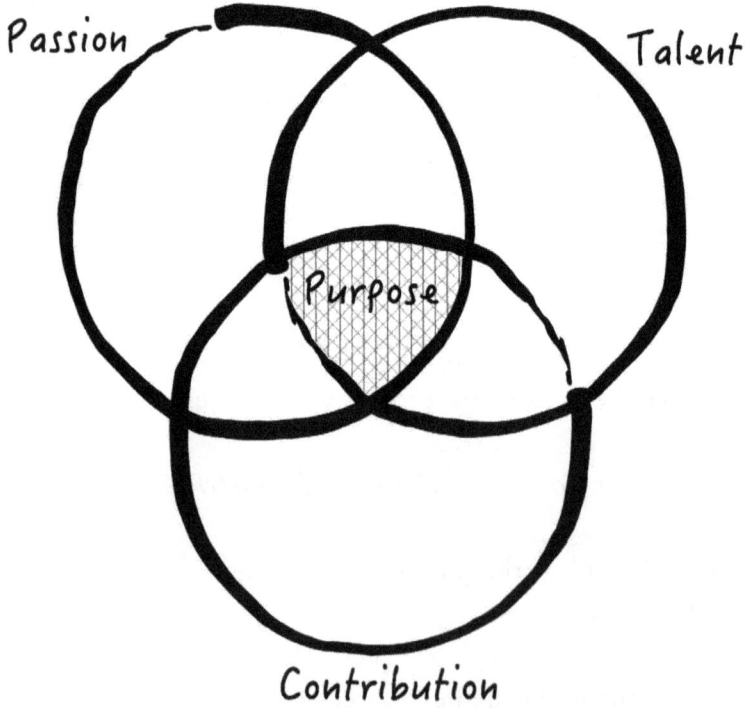

Passion

Talent

Purpose

Contribution

"My Purpose is to

_____   _____   _____
    (verb)   *(object)*   *(impact)*

Through

_____**"**
(The combination between your Passion and Talent)

How do you see the ultimate intersection between all three elements?

How can you contribute toward making the world a slightly better place through this combination of your Passion and Talent?

What is the mission you want to carry out in life that you might realize by doing what you love to do, and what you're great at doing?

Part 3

"Ready to Take Off?"

"I thought this city would be a perfect place where everyone got along and anyone could be anything. Turns out, life's a little bit more complicated than a slogan on a bumper sticker.

Real life is messy.

We all have limitations. We all make mistakes. Which means, hey, glass half full, we all have a lot in common. And, the more we try to understand one another, the more exceptional each of us will be. But, we have to try. So, no matter what kind of person you are, I implore you:
Try.

Try to make the world a better place.

Look inside yourself and recognize that change starts with you.

Judy Hopps (Zootopia, 2016)

Five Ways to Let the Universe Bring You What You Want. Every time.

(originally published on https://medium.com/the-intersection-project)

> *I received a short text from an old friend I hadn't seen in ages: "Just come here and visit us!" Little did I know that this random chat would lead me to a* life-changing *opportunity. Things like this happen too often in my life—coincidentally. Or, do they really?*

Knowing what you want is one thing. But, the journey of getting it is another story. A lot of people say they don't like to be where they are right now. Their work feels dull or meaningless. They get exhausted daily to just barely make enough money every month. Or, their general life conditions drain them or leave them uninspired. But, they don't know how to change their situation.

You feel you're destined to do something more than you're doing now, but you feel trapped. Moving away from something safe is scary. Going into the unknown is risky and terrifying. *It always is*! There's no guarantee things will work out according to plan. In fact, it is guaranteed that things will never go according to plan.

Whenever someone ask me how to start something they have always wanted to do, my answer will depend on the objectives of the question. Are they looking for a practical answer? Or, are they asking out of fear? Are they trying to find reassurance that they will be fine once they take that courageous step?

Practical answers can always be found in books, or in classes, or from any professional consultants. But, reassurance can be only found within one's self. It takes faith to leap into the unknown. It takes a strong belief that, while the path will always be far from smooth, it will be just fine. Because the universe will always help you out. But, only if *you* do the right things to let it do *its* job unexpectedly.

At this time, I had just come back from my one-year responsibility in Cambodia. I had precisely only ten days in Indonesia, before continuing onto my upcoming projects in Taiwan and the Philippines, for three months.

Our large family had just finished a rare big lunch together when I received a short text from a good friend. He informed me there was a conference happening close to where I was. The event was being attended by some great friends I hadn't seen in a while. He then asked me if I would like to come and say hello to the crowd.

It was pretty rare for all of us in the family to be gathered having a fun day out, so I was a bit hesitant to leave them. But, it was a rarer event to be able to meet these friends all at once. Thinking I might not have this chance again for years to come, I finally told my parents I would pay a quick visit, then I'd back with them in no time.

After catching up with my friends at the venue, I decided to take a peek at the main conference hall to see what was happening there. All of a sudden, I recognized a familiar person on the stage. He was delivering a presentation to the audience.

Standing there was a leader I had a lot of respect for, who I had never met in person before. This guy had given me some indirect support throughout my past career on various occasions. He was a person whose famous journey I was aware of, but I'd only had the chance to briefly talk to him through my computer screen.

I went to him after the session just to introduce myself as a random, annoying person who had asked his help in the past. I'm not sure how we got there, but throughout our conversation, I learned he had this dream to start a program to enable young people to discover, and achieve, their dreams. He wanted to keep the ball rolling to make the world a better place. This dream sounded loudly familiar in my head, and in my heart. Because it was also mine!

I didn't even have a tiny clue that our short introductory chat would lead us to working together for our dream just some months later. We eventually worked collaboratively to create and start executing a national-scale program to help young people all over Indonesia discover and develop themselves so they could start their journeys toward contributing positively to their surroundings.

Now that I remember that moment, I can hardly believe how much of a coincidence it was for two people with the same lifelong dreams to meet and finally work together. Everything seemed so random. Everything went so fast. Everything sounded just like a nice coincidence.

I hadn't even planned to go to the conference, nor did I have any idea that my future boss would be there. I also had no clue he'd start a program that resonated with what I had been wanting to do. But, I knew for certain that everything wasn't *just* a coincidence. Things like this happen far too often in my life. Things like wanting something badly then getting it in the most unexpected ways and at an unexpected time.

Some people say I must be very lucky. But, after I experienced things like this so many times, I started to recognize some patterns.

This wasn't luck.

Every single one of us has the power to actively open the window to allow the universe to bring us what we want. And, most importantly, to bring us what we need, every time. Here are some simple steps on how to achieve this.

1. Know exactly what you want AND why you want it

because the universe doesn't want to create random order.

I don't want it to sound like mumbo jumbo, but this is seriously the foremost, fundamental thing we need to ensure the universe conspires to help us. I have no doubt the reason I meet the right opportunity at the right time is by knowing exactly what I want. And, even more importantly, *why* I want it.

One of the problems with people who find it difficult to get what they want is they aren't clear about what they truly want and why they want it. They want life to be better, but in what way? They want to get the opportunity to have a fulfilling career, but what is it that would grant them fulfillment?

It also can be the case that, when they *do* think they know what they want, they don't have a clear reason. They think they want it just because other people tell them so. They think they want it because other people look awesome doing it. For a lot of reasons, humans may never feel enough. Human beings want too many things, endlessly.

You'll be given what you want if, and only if, you know exactly what you want and why you want it. I'm not talking about wanting *that* bag, or *that* car, because your friends have them and they look cool. It is not like wanting a job because your parents say it's good for you.

I'm not talking about desiring an achievement so we can get recognition from others. I'm talking about what *YOU* truly want in life. The one thing you want to fight for, even if it means sacrificing other things. So, before asking how to get what you want, you had better first ask: What do you truly, truly want? Why do you want it? And, does it serve others well?

The universe would love to conspire to help you out if what you desire to do also contributes toward serving others. It knows that every human being should play a role in the grand plan.

This is the start of opening the lock of the window of right opportunities. The starting point of letting the universe do its part. It is also gives us great energy for our second point because — heaven knows — you will need it.

2. Be ready to go ALL OUT

which means: be ready to work crazily hard, while enjoying the journey
with all its ups and downs.

To know is only to begin. To understand what the process will be like is the next step. To be ready to fight and sacrifice is what makes the difference.

A worthwhile journey is always tough. It is dynamic and endless. It can be painful. And it is definitely not for the faint of heart. The right opportunity will only come when we're ready to go all out. It won't come to a person who is unsure about the sacrifice and effort they're willing to make. Also, it won't go to a person who doesn't seem excited about the challenge.

There was a time when I applied for a job opportunity. On paper, I had no doubt I'd make a great candidate. But, the employer decided to choose another candidate who showed more excitement and was ready to give everything. While I, on the other hand, was still unsure. I was considering other opportunities and also had a lot of concerns. I was negotiating with the universe to seek more comfort and an easier path instead of striving. Apparently I wasn't willing to make the sacrifices I needed to make. Later, I understood, it actually all goes back to my point number 1. The job wouldn't have exactly served my ultimate Purpose.

Imagine the universe is like a potential employer and you are applying for a job. Any potential employer only wants to give an opportunity to someone who is fully ready to strive, to fight for the mission, and who is excited about the role. And, that's exactly how the universe chooses when, and to whom, it will give the opportunity.

3. Put yourself out there, let it find you

The universe would not knock on your bedroom door.

I remember the time when I first moved to Bali. Even before I found a place to stay, I was looking for a co-working space.

I've always been clear about what I want to do in life and my reason for doing it. I want to enable young people to discover and design the right, and fulfilling, career path. However, I wasn't clear what would be a suitable channel by which to pursue what I wanted. Then I went to the perfect place to allow the universe to find me.

A co-working space is, by far, the best platform for me to interact with various types of careers and be in touch with a community of diverse professionals from different backgrounds. It is also an awesome place to meet with unexpected opportunity. It is definitely a place well-suited to exploration, learning, and being surprised.

It was a late afternoon when I was having a casual chat with an architect/artist, whom I had just met, on the balcony of the co-working space. I told her I had an idea to produce a creative facilitation book for young adults. Then, within only a couple of days, she had introduced me to some of her friends.

One thing led to another. She put me in contact with one of her old friends: a person who had a similar aspiration to contribute to the process of shaping the future generation. A strong individual who I now call my writing partner in The Intersection Project.

It was the beginning of the most exciting journey I've had to date. And I definitely would not have got such an opportunity if I had just isolated myself in my room, at my individual working desk. We always need to put ourselves out there, where the universe brings opportunity right in front of our noses.

4. Know when to say 'No' and when to say 'Yes'

because there will always be temptation.

Once you put yourself out there for the universe to find you, there will be a time when you are offered tons of various opportunities. If you are like me, sometimes you may have the tendency to bite off more than you can chew. The opportunities may *all* look great. We can get pumped up to take on all of them. We think we are great at multi-tasking anyway, so juggling roles will be exciting rather than difficult.

However, we should be aware that saying 'yes' to temptation can lead us further from what we intend to achieve. Not only can it put our main goals on hold, it can also decrease our initial energy and motivation. And, even scarier, it can get us off track.

It doesn't mean you can strictly only do one thing at a time. People have different conditions and circumstances. It is nonsense to tell someone to just quit their job when they need to provide food for their families. Sometimes juggling things is inevitable, and that's okay. There are great entrepreneurs who juggle their 9-to-5 job with their skill-learning time in the evening, during their early years.

What makes the right opportunity different from temptation is the aim it serves. Temptation will always serve the short term goal. It looks easy in the beginning, but it has the possibility of trapping you in a comfort zone where you are shifted further from your initial Purpose.

Right opportunities might require a lot of work but they would be in line with your long-term goal. The journey will grant you the equipment you need along the way. It will also open other doors, through building the right networks, developing new skills, while strengthening your initial motivation. And, most importantly, a right opportunity should align with your core values.

Be courageous to say 'No' to temptation, so the universe can bring you the right opportunities to lead you to your ultimate goals.

5. Listen to the signs, and take the leap

Imagine you're playing a video game. You're the main actor, on a quest to find a treasure. In the quest you will meet people, you will go places, and you will find clues. These things have a role: they are signs to get you closer to the treasure you seek.

I take the 'everything happens for a reason' phrase pretty literally. To some extent, the universe communicates through small signs. And, these signs lead me to an unexpected opportunity, if—and only if—I have the courage to leap.

Signs can form in something we see, hear, or experience. They come when you already have the right questions in mind and you are actively seeking for answers. They come when you know exactly what you want but are still unsure about how to get it. They come when you are ready to fight in your quest for your treasure.

Always ask. Look around. Listen. Then take the leap.

Behind every warrior, there is always an army. There is no way a champion can win the battle all by themselves. Even when you think you're walking alone on a road less traveled, have faith that you are not. When you fight for the right thing, the universe will always conspire to help you. It always comes when you are ready. When you have clarity of reason. When you are ready to fight and to sacrifice. It comes when you are ready to commit to taking the endless quest. It comes when you need guards to protect your dreams.

Be clear and be still. But, be open at the same time, because the universe conspires and shows you the way in the most unexpected manner.

Chapter 8

Foreseeing the Future

Before starting any journey, we need to understand where we are now, the destination we want to reach, and which path we want to take. Before you start your endless journey in living a fulfilling life, the first task you should accomplish is to know your destination and which journey you want to pursue.

As we have seen in earlier chapters, a career takes up a huge portion of our lives, and it is also natural for human beings to experience joy from contributing something positive to their surroundings. Therefore, aligning the right type of career with your life's Purpose will clearly bring happiness while, at the same time, improve society. Discovering your purposeful career is not like reading about job openings in a newspaper or on any website. Your purposeful career could be a popular job in your society, but it could also be something you've never heard of before; or it could even be the type of career that has never existed before.

Discovering your purposeful career is, in a way, about designing the type of career and activity you want to do while also understanding how you can make a living out of it. A purposeful career is what you continually do in life. It is not the title you hold nor the name of a job position that is assigned to you. It is about the alignment between what your heart wants to fight for, and the exploration of ideas, resulting in concrete actions as the output. It is about what you create through the collaboration of your soul, your mind, and your concrete actions.

Envisioning Your Purposeful Career

In order to design your purposeful career, first and foremost allow us to zoom in on the area of Contribution. This process will help you envision what you actually desire to see in your surroundings—the state of the issues you care about—in the distant future.

1st Activity

Estimated Duration: 30 minutes
(including time for journaling)

1. Allocate some time where you can be in a place, and in a condition, where you have zero distraction for approximately 30 minutes.
2. When you are ready, close your eyes and be in a state of meditation where you can focus on your deep breathing. Focus on the air circulation. Also, let your senses be aware of the sounds around you.
3. Visualize a condition that you think is the most ideal state for the issue you deeply care about: the issue you want to make Contribution to. Spend some time there. Imagine you're watching a short film. What images do you see?

Journaling :

Feel free to describe what you just visualized by any method you're most comfortable with.

Be specific:

What did you see?

Who were the subjects, or the actors?

What did you hear?

How did you feel?

The state you just visualized is the destination you want to reach. It may seem huge and it may seem impossible to achieve. The truth is, you *may* achieve it, but also you may not achieve it in one lifetime. It may need the next generation to carry the mission forward. It doesn't matter whether you will—or won't—be able to see that vision turn into a reality before your eyes. What matters is that this destination has the power to be your aspiration. This aspiration will keep you going no matter what. It can help you find the fuel you need on this long road.

The clearer your destination is, the more powerful and long lasting it can become. Therefore, try to form the images you visualize into one clear statement, consisting of a clear subject—the group of people you want to impact—and how you envision their condition to be. The following is an example of my destination:

People in their twenties to thirties are fulfilled in their careers because they understand they are doing what they really want to do in life in order to contribute to the improvement of the world

Now that you have the ideal vision for your surroundings, it is time for you to visualize your future self. The next activity will help you envision the career that will bring ongoing fulfillment in your life.

2nd *Activity*

Estimated Duration: 30 minutes (including time for journaling)

1. Go back to your state of meditation, where you can feel completely calm and comfortable. Activate your senses. Be fully present and take time to focus on your breathing.

2. Recall the previous images you had in mind when you saw the ideal condition appear before your eyes; where you felt really good about what was happening around the situation.

3. Pay attention to the previous images, as if you were holding a camera to capture the situation. Imagine you're slowly turning the camera around. Someone else is now holding a camera to capture *YOU* and your activities in that same film.

Journaling:

Feel free to describe what you just visualized by any method you're most comfortable with.

Try to be specific:

What did you see yourself doing?

_____

_____

_____

_____

_____

What role did you play in making the condition evolve positively?

_____

_____

_____

_____

_____

How would you feel doing these activities? Would it give you a
sense of joy and satisfaction if you did them repeatedly?

How would it make you feel if you got validation through seeing
results, or progressive improvement, in the issue you are working
on?

Remember: what you saw *could* be your professional career.
How do you see these activities providing you with
a financial income?

We are getting closer to defining your career vision and finally achieving clarity on the path you are going to pursue. On the template below, list the activities you were doing in the preceding visualization as part of your purposeful career. Try to see what is the main theme of these activities? What is similar in the actions you see yourself doing? If there are some specific numbers that appear in your visualization, state them as well in your career vision.

The continual, and diverse, activities I can do as part of my purposeful career are :

1. _____

2. _____

3. _____

4. _____

5. _____

Here's an example:

The continual, and diverse, activities I can do as part of my purposeful career are:
- Training, and workshop delivery
- One-on-one coaching toward self-discovery and career path design
- Public speaking
- Writing books

> The main theme of these activities is :

Here's an example:

The main theme of these activities is:
 I facilitate young people to discover their true purpose

> Career Vision :
>
> Through my   I can

Here's an example:

Career Vision :
 Through my facilitating I can enable 1 million people to live
 their purposeful careers.

To strengthen your vision, it is highly suggested you have this statement printed or written on a piece of paper that you can take with you everywhere. Or, you can also attach it in places where you can see it every day.

This career vision will be the basic framework of your career path. It is not a goal. It is not a trophy to compete for. It will be a reminder. A reminder for you, and for us, to design and live the path that aligns with Purpose. It is also, in a way, your 'Calling'.

Chapter 9

Tools for the Warrior

Some might say this is a fun rollercoaster ride. A road less traveled. A marathon. An adventure. But, there's one thing we need to remember: it is also a continuous war, and you are the warrior.

Along the way, you will realize the toughest opponent you will fight against is none other than yourself. Failures may come, challenges are always around the corner, temptations will appear in different disguises, but it is your actions that always matter: your responses to tough conditions; your decisions in choosing one option out of the many; and your attitude in dealing with breakdowns. It requires another level of awareness and determination to always choose the brave actions, and to fight anything that might lure you into giving up.

To win the battle, a warrior always needs to equip themselves with a set of tools. These tools will help you to always win: to choose courage, to build your skills, and to form a strong support system.

Acknowledging Fear and Choosing Courage

Try to think about one particular person you know who has no fear of anything. I bet finding their name is as easy as finding a needle in a haystack. If, after defining your career vision statement, you feel excited and can't wait to start your journey, congratulations, you are moving in the right direction! And, if you feel excited and also scared at the same time, do not worry, because you are definitely not alone.

Having fear is inevitable. Having fear is human and there's nothing wrong with that. A great fear of losing someone is a reminder that person is important to you. Having fear of doing something can also be a sign that the thing you want to do is really important to you, and may also be for the rest of the world. Nothing is wrong with having fear. What *is* wrong with fear is when you let it stop you doing what you're supposed to do, or being what you're supposed to become.

> *"Making a big life changing decision is pretty scary,*
> *but, know what's even scarier? Regret."*
> Zig Ziglar

Fear can't be ignored but it can be managed. In order to know how to overcome your fear and decide to choose courage, you need to first acknowledge the true fear. What is actually your biggest concern in living your purposeful path? What scares you in taking the journey? Is it the fear of disappointment you might get from your loved ones? Is it a financial concern? Or, is it the thought of not feeling good enough to perform such a mission? What is the root cause of these concerns? What is your ultimate fear?

My friend, let's call her Mandy, has a great heart for community development. What she is currently striving for is definitely not an easy and smooth journey. She came from a society where her close friends and family expected her to get security from a high paying job in a multinational company. With her academic background in Business Management, she has always had great ideas and plans, but at the same time, she has had massive fear in executing them. As a perfectionist, her fear has always been complicated, yet valid: from fear of financial instability, or her own capacity in enabling other communities to thrive; or fear of being alone and misunderstood. But, her greatest deep-rooted fear is actually the fear of rejection.

As a former straight-A student, Mandy has a desire for her efforts to be accepted by the community. It's difficult for her to imagine the possibility of her plans being rejected. An even bigger fear of rejection comes from her loved ones. Mandy has always wanted to make her parents proud. She knows that her parents have invested a lot in her education so she can have a prestigious job and live a safe life. Mandy also knows that she thinks differently than her friends in her social circle, who perceive joining the corporate world as the best option. She is scared she will be judged as naïve or pretentious whenever she wants to share her thoughts about bringing a positive impact to society. At the beginning—and it still arises during challenging times—the solitary path scared her.

It took time, endless reading, and continual conversations with the right type of people for Mandy to understand she had the full right to live the kind of life she wanted. It became crystal clear to her that what was most important is her *own* belief, not that of others. She had faith that what she was doing was bringing positive improvement to the society she cared about. Mandy knew the journey was difficult and no one could guarantee she'd be successful, but she believed in her Purpose and that God would lead her on her way.

Knowing your ultimate fear is one thing, but understanding it is different. After accepting and acknowledging the existence of your fear and not hating yourself for having one—or two, or five—you also need to understand the reason for its existence. In other words, understand how your fear was born. There are various reasons for fear, which also means there are different ways to overcome it.

Initial fear is a type of fear that everyone has in normal doses—such as fear of falling when you go to a high building, or of being alone in the dark—but it can be something much more complex, like a phobia, which we might need further psychological assistance to overcome.

Fear of rejection—what Mandy had—can be classified as initial fear, but it can also be something else. During our over-coffee conversation—eventually expanded into an interview for this book—Mandy told me that, when she was a child, there was a period of time when her older sister didn't want to be in the same room as her. More than a decade later, Mandy finally understood that her sister had just needed some privacy in dealing with her teenage life. But, Mandy didn't know that back then, nor did her sister, who had never experienced such confusion before.

What Mandy remembered was only the mild pain of being rejected by the person she looked up to. She loved her sister dearly and had never hated or gotten angry with her for what happened in the past, since she had thought it was insignificant anyway. She never thought this small condition would shape her character and the way she perceived the world. But, it did. She hadn't realized that such a bad experience had traumatized her and given her a deep-rooted fear of rejection.

Her perfectionism and doubting her capacity were also caused by a similar event. It grew from her childhood experience, when her mom wasn't satisfied with her grades when she got less than eight out of ten in her tests. There is always a part of her ego that automatically says she is never good enough. It took years for Mandy to finally understand the root cause of her fear, and to manage it throughout the dynamic process of her current, purposeful career journey.

It is rare for an individual to have a perfect childhood. At some point, it leaves scars that we bring into adulthood. The first step to overcome the type of fear caused by a bad past experience is to accept that it happened, and understand that it also might have needed to happen at that time to teach you a lesson.

You can also be at peace with it by forgiving the past—it can be a person or the circumstances—and also to be grateful for it having played a certain role in your life. It might have given you a realization how to strive for excellence or how to be careful and better prepared; or how to forgive others sincerely. Try to always believe that whatever happened to you played a beneficial role in your growth, no matter how painful it was. Once you can be at peace with your bad past experiences, or simply be mindful that you want to progress in being at peace with them, you will understand that fear is not a brick wall hindering you from living a fulfilling life.

Aside from growing out of bad past experiences, fear can also be formed and constructed by a number of external perceptions. We live, and are raised, in a social environment where other people's perspectives, and certain cultures, subconsciously bring certain understandings to our mind.

We sometimes forget that most of the time we can't see things in black and white. Opinions are opinions. But, we shouldn't decide what is wrong or right based on what our society thinks. External perception can bring positive reminders sometimes, but it can also bring too many restrictions for us to achieve what we truly think is important.

In some cultures, society may have a concept of what a successful life should be like. In eastern cultures, people in their mid-twenties are perceived to be successful if they have a stable job and income, have started to invest, have some assets, and have got married and had kids.

It seems like the whole life of one human being is already in a framework ever since they entered the academic world. It is framework that is full of syllabuses and 'dos and don'ts'. According to this framework of thought, there is no space for self-exploration, the adventurous path, and trial and error. It seems like there is no time for the excitement of the unknown and for failure: that need for people to let things happen in order for them to understand what truly brings fulfillment in their lives. It's not that it's wrong to take the safe path, but sometimes avoiding risks in life can produce the biggest risk of all time: regret for not trying.

In speaking of the pile of external perceptions, I remember having a conversation with my Dad and my sister over breakfast. My sister asked my Dad whether he'd ever had any concern about the life choices his two daughters had made so far, which might be perceived as different from what's normal in our extended family and society. My Dad answered: "Life is not like playing chess, there is no exact step or rigid format in living life. I trust both of you will make the right decisions in living a life that you love." And, that's why I love my Dad.

So, in the end, when you have acknowledged and understood the existence of your deepest fear, it is completely your decision if you want to let your fear grow stronger and defeat you, or if you want to choose courage over fear. Here are a few methods to *courageously* choose courage:

1. Consciously training the attitude of optimism can be one of the ways to choose courage. Whenever you worry and ask, What if I fail?, turn the question into: What if I succeed?, and you will see how positivity can drive you further beyond your expectations.

2. Sometimes fear exists not to block you from achieving what you want, it can also be a gentle reminder for you to be careful and prepare better. Being solution-oriented means understanding a potential problem and getting ready to face it in the wisest way possible, while also training yourself always to be ready to face the unexpected. Rather than cancelling your plan to go out because you're afraid it might rain, you'd better bring an umbrella or a raincoat so you will be able to enjoy your outing under the raindrops.

3. Having clarity of Purpose will help you go beyond what you could ever imagine. There isn't any easy journey in taking a purposeful path, but when you trust you are doing something good—with

good intentions, continuous real effort, and hard work— support and help will come from different corners, in a most unexpected form and at the right time.

4.   Finally, the most important step in choosing courage over fear of the unknown is to directly face it. Equip yourself with the three weapons just listed above, take a step, press the START button and you'll be impressed at how you are able to face these challenges.

Building the Needed Skills

Having a vision of what you want to see in your surroundings, and in the world, gives you the fuel to always move forward on the endless road. Having a vision of your career gives you a clear idea of where you want to go and what you ultimately want to do in life. This is the amazing start of your journey. Clarity is crucial because, if you really want something in life, the universe will conspire to show you the way.

While waiting for the universe to open the unexpected door, a wise man will not just wait for magic to happen and do nothing. Understanding Passion and Talent is a great asset, but it won't give any guarantee you will achieve what you want. It is definitely not a magic door, but it is a map by which to find your treasure.

In order for you to get closer to your career vision, you need to have the capacity to do so. Any great career needs a marvelous set of skills that can't only be learned in a classroom. They need to be experienced. It takes time, continual effort, and persistence to build the skills you need. Mastery is an imaginary finish line. The more you know, the more you understand you still need to learn more. There is no single point in your life when you are able to say: "I have enough learning; I have mastered this". Developing yourself is an endless process, and that's the beauty of life.

> *Formal Learning – Interaction - Experience*
> *TO KNOW – TO UNDERSTAND – TO BE ABLE*

The process of learning and self-development is always a combination of formal process, direct interaction, and experience. While it is important to understand some theories and basic concepts through formal learning—such as school, training, or reading material—this would only provide the basic knowledge. Direct interaction through coaching, mentoring, feedback processes, group discussion, or something as simple as a conversation with people who have already had the experience before you, is the second level of learning.

Effective listening with empathy will help you to understand the real work in the field. Attentive listening will stimulate your mind to actively analyze conditions and generate more curiosity which leads to follow-up questions and a further level of discussion. In this process you will see the power of questioning and deep conversation. It will appear in the form of butterflies in your stomach, sparks in your eyes, and those flashlights in your brain that show you've been enlightened.

Do you need to delay the beginning of your purposeful career journey until you have mastered these skills? No, you'd better start as soon as possible. In fact, you can start from now. The highest level of learning is through experiencing it directly. Skills can be developed along the way and be sharpened each day.

You can be a better public speaker by being on stage speaking, getting feedback from an audience, evaluating yourself, then going back to the stage, and repeating the process all over again. You can be a better writer by writing every single day. You know you cannot be better in drawing without taking your pencil to, or scratching that pen on, a piece of paper. In any skill you want to master, you need to go to the field, get your hands dirty, and continually train your muscles. And, this includes experiencing failure, appreciating the pain, and then getting up once again in a better way.

The Power of a Supportive Environment

If you think your career vision is close to impossible—it both excites you and scares you at the same time—then you are on the right path. It is normal not to know how you will be able to reach it. Realizing that you will enter the unknown once you decide to take this journey is crucial. It means you will allow surprises along the way and understand that not everything will go according to your plan; but, no matter what, it will be even better than your own plan. To allow for this to happen, there needs to be diverse involvement from different parties along the way.

No matter how capable we are as an individual, we know we will never be able to do big things by ourselves. We always need other people—lots of people—to either collaborate, mentor us, open those unexpected doors, or give a different form of support at the time we need it the most. Therefore, before starting the journey of your purposeful career, it is extremely important for you to understand the power of a supportive environment and know where you want to place yourself.

Up to this point, it is crystal-clear that a purposeful journey is always far from easy; but it's definitely worth it. Having the right people around you is one of the crucial factors in helping you to stay on track, in quickening the process, or in expanding your reach and impact.

Your Supportive Environment

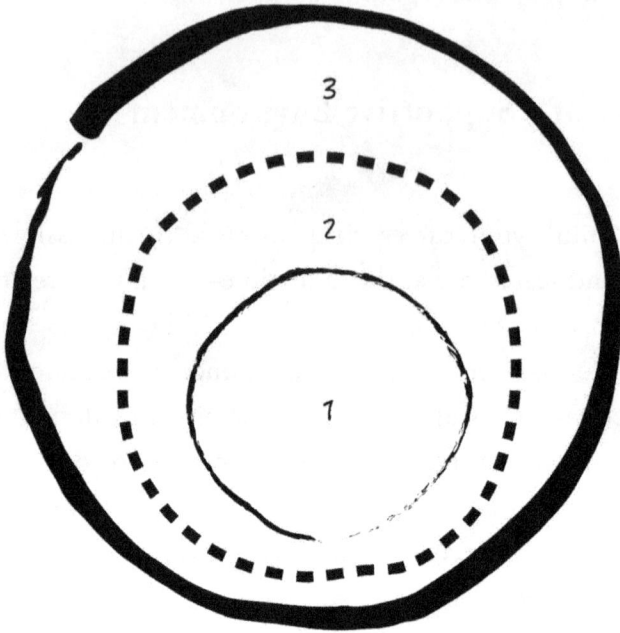

The Circles:

(1) The closest circle you need to build in your purposeful career journey is a small group of people to collaborate with professionally. It can be a partner, or a small team consisting of people with an aligned vision, or it might be a mentor. Remember how your destination can be a fuel during this endless journey? It is the same with your team: they will need clarity of Purpose and vision to ensure you can go down this road less traveled, hand in hand, together. Having a mentor or coach for personal-professional development is also a strong support system in living a purposeful career.

This first circle should be filled with those people you can fully trust: who you will talk to closely, regularly, and endlessly. They are the people with whom you think you can exponentially develop yourself. With them you will have ongoing, in-depth conversations regarding your career and mission.

(2) The second circle represents the type of environment where you can interact with like-minded people who you can continually approach for various reasons, whether it be for brainstorming or external feedback: such as getting a second opinion when your team needs input on your current hypothesis, or being in contact with their network when you need external collaboration. This is an environment where you may find endless unexpected opportunities coming from different corners that will help you to reach your destination in a way you couldn't think of before.

Trust me, once you are in the right group, or community, or environment, the level of surprise will be intense. The door of opportunity, which might just appear before you during one random chat on a balcony, could change your life forever. Do you know why these things happen? Once you are clear in your Purpose, your words will portray it, your eyes will speak about your desire to bring positive evolution to your environment, and your positive energy will fill the atmosphere surrounding you. This will make it difficult for the right people to avoid helping you— even strangers who might have the capacity to do so.

Try to think strategically. If you're into art, surround yourself with different types of artists, or people from the art industry. If you want to be a technopreneur, be in a community full of IT people. If you need to improve your skills and be accomplished in one particular area, the community that can help you thrive should be filled with people from the same profession.

However, in most of cases, it is also important to be in a community with a diverse profile, background, and professional base, so you are able to access and be exposed to a broad network with an unknown limitation, and always able to get insight from diverse perspectives when you need it. To have both characters in one community, or to be able to access different types of communities according to your needs, will help you proceed faster than you might have previously expected.

The most important thing to assess the right type of environment you should put yourself in is how much the people inside it are willing to support each other, and possibly collaborate, if any alignment occurs in the future. The result could even be beyond your expectation if they also have their own mission: if they already have clarity on their Purpose and what they want to fight for. Even though each person in the group does a different thing, you would know that, indirectly, you are working in collaboration to make the world slightly better.

Ideally, you need to have regular and direct physical interaction. Since we all know the path we take is not easy, actively involving yourself in this supportive environment will make your journey feel less lonely. You can also have more than one community with different characters and purposes. One thing to remember, in this environment, is that you will also need to be an active and supportive element. The more you're willing to support other members in the group, the more doors will unexpectedly open for you

(3) The outer circle, the biggest circle, represents those people who will continually offer tremendous support and positive energy, especially at the moment you need it most. It might consist of the same people as in the second circle, but it can also be a completely different group. These people might not even understand exactly

what it is you're doing, what you're talking about (although they definitely try their best to understand, or at least listen attentively), and what keeps you up at night. But, these are the people who believe in you, who trust you're making the right decisions in choosing this path.

They believe what you are fighting for is important and they are ready to support you in any way within their capacity. If they think you have a different perspective, they will be proud of you for being special. Though they know your vision *seems* impossible, they believe you are able to get closer to it every single day. In some circumstances, these are the people who will also be open to challenging your thoughts—rather than blocking you—and helping you to see from different perspectives to broaden your view.

This group of people can consist of your parents, your brother or sister, your lover, or your best friends who might live in a different city, or continent. Having these people will provide the right positive energy for you to keep on striving. They know you so well they are always ready to remind you about your potential and capability when you are in doubt or feel scared. Being on this road less traveled can be difficult and exhausting, but having positive people around will definitely help you enjoy this journey worth living.

Taking a road less traveled will need serious commitment and a good deal of preparation. It will not be like that two-week vacation break where you know you will be back home soon, no matter how amazing or terrible the trip is. It is also not a random trial of subscription you can just cancel if it doesn't work out. It is, instead, a long and endless— but worthwhile—adventure with a clear objective and Purpose. Therefore, before taking off, it is crucial to understand the direction you are heading in and the most likely obstacles along the way. In facing the ongoing battle, every warrior needs his tools. These are the tools you will use to design your purposeful path and, later, to support you in walking on the fateful road.

Chapter 10

Designing Your Authentic Path

Though it would be nice to stop at merely knowing what your career vision is, the journey of living a purposeful career doesn't just end with a statement. Getting to know your vision is only the beginning of this endless path you'll be taking. It should be followed by the understanding that you have everything you need to design your own authentic path.

In Chapter 4, I shared the common pattern I noticed in numerous purposeful career journeys. The pattern came from observing different professions with a variety of expertise and backgrounds, but they all had one strong common trait. They were using their clarity of Purpose, both at the beginning, *and* as the main driver along the way. Based on the stories that they've told, and been living, there are some inevitable similarities which can't be ignored.

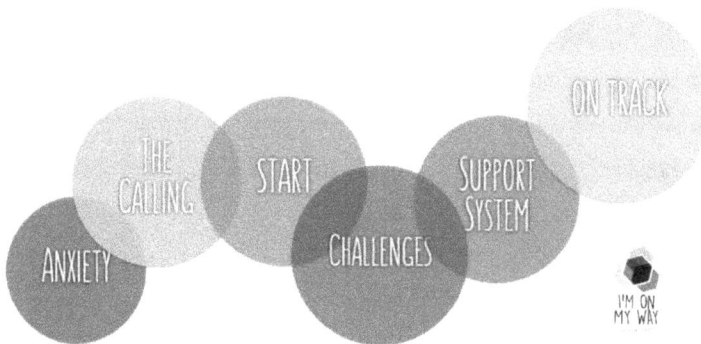

While any purposeful career path has this endless roller-coaster ride pattern in common, none of them are identical. In fact, every path is always different.

Their stages are not in any rigid linear order. In a lot of cases they go continually back and forth, finding their way back on track whenever they go slightly off. Even though things will never go exactly as planned, it is still crucial to design our own authentic path to keep us on track.

Writing your career vision will take you to the second stage. By now, you will have passed the anxiety of not knowing—or being unsure about—who you are and/or the role you should be playing. By now, you will have found your 'calling'.

It is the moment to decide when, and where, to start. It is also the time when you can define when and how you will utilize your warrior tools to start winning the endless battle.

You may start to think that, by the end of this book, you'll have a detailed roadmap. Unfortunately, that will not be the case. This chapter will not provide a comprehensive goal-setting template. We will not be designing the path via a complicated chart filled with MOS and KPI. We will not create a path that looks like any fancy business plan.

Mapping out the whole framework and deciding the first steps are crucial. At the same time, however, we also need to allow some room for the universe to play its role of giving you nice surprises along the way. What we will be doing in the next few minutes or so, will be creating the perfect setting for the universe to do its job.

Sketching Out the Marathon Path

In the previous process, we successfully visualized the ideal future we would like to see. It is the destination we're longing to reach. It is our aspiration for the surroundings that we care about. It is our long-term dream. It is located way above the current reality we are living in.

There is no guarantee there will be a moment when we can touch it with our bare hands. One thing is certain: we want to contribute to that long winding journey in order to get closer to that aspiration.

Therefore, we also have a career vision: the picture of an ideal condition, specifically for us. A career vision establishes a condition where we feel fulfilled through living the right type of career, one that is not defined by a position in a single hierarchy, but by a set of activities that resonates closely to our being. A career that sounds authentic to our soul.

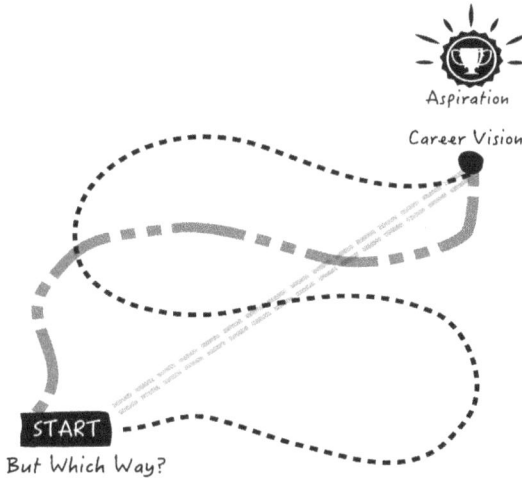

A career vision will put us on the right path toward contributing to our aspiration. What we concretely have—at this very moment—is the 'Now'. Having a future aspiration is great, but the things we concretely do each day are what will bridge the reality gap. This is exactly what we are sketching out right now.

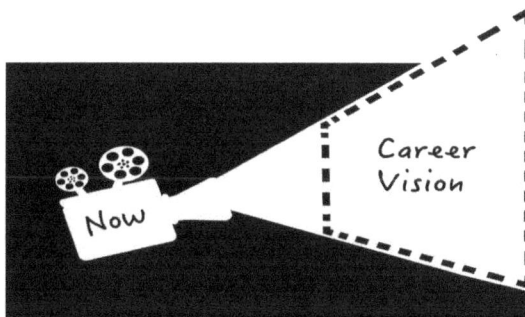

Writing down the practical steps toward achieving a conventional professional ambition is like asking people to stand in line in front of a cashier. Clear, straight to the point, easy, and—well—practical. You can find the answer through reading the right book, or even one single article, or by talking to some professionals in a particular field. Then, voila! You will have your list of milestones to achieve in some expected timeline.

However, our design work will look nothing like a plan to get the 'Best Salesman in Asia-Pacific' award. We also will not be talking about how to write an appealing résumé, or tips and tricks for a successful interview, or how to close the deal.

Our path will look nothing like clear steps on how to be a Senior Marketing Manager in 3 years. We're talking about non-hierarchical career paths here. We're designing paths that may not have existed in any job practice before.

We might be designing *your* authentic path on the issue of 'how to play sports to combat discrimination', or toward 'financial consultancy to support the sustainability of community development'. It might be directed at 'how to improve a human's productivity and efficiency through product design', or even 'how to explore the ocean while enabling healthy environmental tourism'. Or mapping out a track toward 'leading a team in creating disruptive change in our education system'.

You might find some scanty ideas on how to succeed in a particular area through reading particular writings, but you won't have your plan set in one go by copying another person's track. Your path will be unique and dynamic. It will be yours, and yours alone.

You are the designer and the executor. There is nothing at all conventional about designing the path to fit your authentic, fulfilling, and purposeful career—let alone living it.

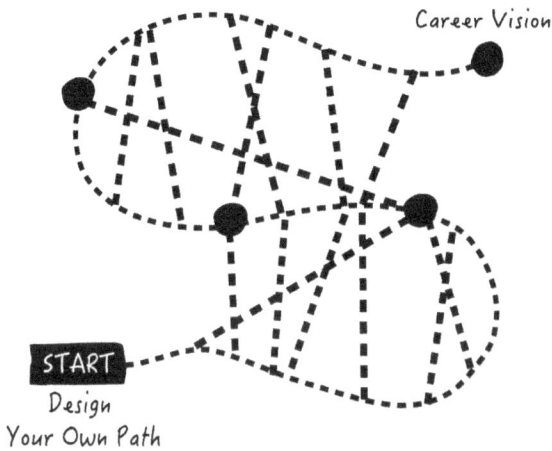

Career Vision

START
Design
Your Own Path

Now that we are on the same page, we will proceed to the design process. Here's how it goes. Our main objective is not to create action steps to cover the next ten years. Because, let's face it, even within the next single month, there will be at least one unexpected circumstance that will happen in your life: an unexpected condition that may either accelerate, or put any of your plans on hold. Therefore, rather than finding yourself having to throw away your grand 'to-do list' next week—just like that New Year resolution that is hidden somewhere by mid-January—we want to have a more practical outcome.

By the end of this chapter, it is expected you will know the areas you need to focus on in the next one to three months—and, how to do so. However, in order to arrive at that result, we will need to map out the whole long-term career framework. The design of our path will be like a sketch of an endless marathon, and we will now prepare your very first lap.

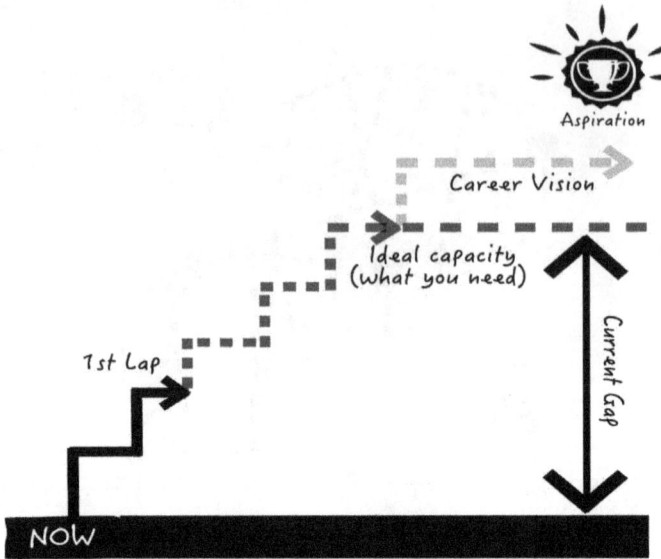

1. Destination

   Written as the lifelong aspiration, 'destination' will play its role as a reminder. It will remind you of the future ideal state you want to see: the dream you may not achieve fully in one lifetime. It is the dream that will become your legacy, where you will contribute in getting closer to it. It will be the push whenever your motivation is low or when you start questioning the career you have chosen and the Purpose you have defined. It is the reason why you will always want to keep going.

2. Career Vision

   This works as the basic framework of your career path. Stating your vision and the activities you intend to use as your channels will set the right tone. It draws the lines of the wider track. Since it is impossible for your path to consist of a clear line and rigid steps, your career vision should define a spacious area where you are still on the right track. Therefore, it will allow you to do various activities and explorations, while you are still in that area of your career vision. It will also enable you to see the big picture that may cover your entire lifetime. You will see that it is not only a job. You will see that you are working for a mission, one that also happens to enable you to make a living out of it.

3. What You Need

This section will guide you in seeing all the things you need to get closer to your career vision. They are the ideal circumstances that will enable you to proceed on the right track: the things you need to support you in doing the activities that align with your career vision.

4. The Now

At this stage, we will need to be grounded to see our current reality as it is. We will assess the things we already have at present, so we will able to see the gap between what we *need* to have and what we *do* have in order to eventually know how to bridge it.

Besides assessing what we have, we also need to see the circumstances we are in right now. This will help us to decide whether we are ready to fight full time, or need longer preparation through taking a temporary, part-time focus. We will also predict the signs and symptoms, showing when we will be ready to transition to full-time focus.

5. Your 1st Lap

Depending on the time you can commit in the next one-to-three months, here we will design some practical things you can do. We are going to design the early action steps needed to bridge the gap in order to make your start outstanding. This will be your very first step in the endless exciting journey of a purposeful career.

The Ideal Circumstances

There was an occasion when I joined a writers' meetup. In a room full of creative writers, authors, and journalists, we discussed how to build a successful writing routine. One author shared a challenge he'd found at home. He'd experienced a major irritation because, whenever he would start getting into his writing flow, his wife would disturb his zone. Almost all the participants nodded together in agreement, including me.

One female novelist then told us about a piece she had read once. She said that in order to write a book or create a story, an author needs to enter a completely different world. And, in order to go to that other dimension, we need to create a gate in the form of a specific situation that will enable us to go into that flow. Some people said they would need particular music; others admitted they needed aromatherapy. Knowing how much of an effort the process of entering that gate was, authors would certainly find it upsetting when someone went ahead and cut the flow, because it meant they would need to rebuild the gate all over again.

I have a specific way to build and construct *my* 'gate'. As a frequent daydreamer, my perfect condition is writing alone on a balcony where I can have a full panoramic view. Unfortunately, this is only a once in a while condition for me. On normal days, I need to substitute it with something else. If I have to write in a busy place, I would need a space in a corner, to feel 'safe' from the possibility of people taking a glimpse at my screen; but also one that enables me to observe people all across the room. I would need the table and chair to be at a particular height. I would also need a soothing playlist on my earphones. I would definitely need a cup of coffee, almost every time. Lately, I also realized that a certain room temperature plays an important role in setting the right atmosphere. It sounds pretty demanding, I know. But, all these conditions make the ideal environment for me to pass the gate: to enter my flow.

Just like in constructing a gate to let writers enter another world, we also all need to build certain circumstances to enable us to live a purposeful career. Our career vision might seem far distant and close to impossible but predicting the set of ideal conditions to enable us to live that vision, is indeed feasible, and practical.

This situation might vary from one person to another. It depends on the area and sector we want to work in and the scope of the impact we want to create. It also even depends on our nature, or personality. A person who is highly driven by challenge and competition might find it difficult to be productive in a rather serene setting. A person who is favored with dynamism and flexibility would feel drained in a rigid system, strictly controlled by regulation. Every person has their own set of conditions that can enable them to run extra miles on a purposeful career track.

These ideal circumstances can include—but are not limited to— the areas of:

- skills and knowledge
- the type of network
- the working environment and social environment
- resources

These are the things you need. They should be the circumstances that can enable you to thrive. They are there to help you perform your mission, not feed human desire.

Picturing Your Gate

Estimated Duration: 15 minutes

Take a look at your career vision statement and also the activities you want to do to channel its delivery. Imagine one ideal condition that might enable you to achieve excellence. What are the things you need? What does your gate look like? Try to be as detailed as possible without thinking too much about how you would get there. We will explore the technicalities of 'how' in a different section. Try to ask the following questions of yourself to start envisioning your gate:

What are the skills you need to execute these activities?

Do you need to be great at marketing, or sales? Do you need to be good at writing, or making videos? Do you need to be awesome at public speaking? People say that a networking skill is at the core of advancing your career, is it also relevant to your need? Do you need any technical skills to support your plan?
What is the knowledge you need to have?

What are the type of networks you would need in order to be connected to limitless opportunities?

What are the networks that could accelerate the process of realizing your vision and excelling in the impact?
Is it the government? Youth communities? The media?
What type of network can you see as opening up an opportunity for collaboration?

What kind of working conditions would you thrive in?

Imagine an ideal working culture that would work best for you. You can refer back to the core values that you hold on to and also your personality traits. Also, imagine the type of social connection—the support system—you would need to thrive. Remember that we are the reflections of the closest people around us. They could affect how we think and how we make decisions in life.

What are the resources you would need to realize your vision?

Would you need a team to work together? How would you define your ideal team? Are there any other assets you would need to function effectively?

After reflecting on the questions above, try to define the construction of the ideal gate that could lead you to your career vision.

You may describe it in any way you want, as long as you can refer back to it anytime you need. This image of your ideal circumstances is critical in continuing to the following steps.

Clarity of the Present

Since you are already well-connected with your Purpose, I have no doubt you are prepared to do whatever it takes to start living it. While determination can be driven from within, circumstances come as inevitable variables that can't be ignored. Especially at the moment we want to start, circumstances that come our way can be a major pain in the neck. They can resist our starting what we are destined to do. Anything can be on the list: an accident, someone's death, the need to provide food for our family, an urgent medical procedure, or the infamous 'I don't have the money to start' statement. The list can be as long as the Great Wall of China.

Rather than fighting the reality and thinking we are doomed, we'd better have the mentality that the situation is not *that* special. It's undeniable that every champion has to go through tough circumstances at the beginning of their battle. They can even continue along the way, endlessly. Do they therefore stop striving? Well, they might have fear and doubt, but they keep on going regardless.

We are not victims in having challenges. The first thought we need to have is to stop asking 'Why did it happen?" and start asking 'What now?' What we can do is to assess our situation objectively. What we can do is to see it as it is. Only through understanding it, can we make the wise decision to start what we want to start—no matter what.

What You Have

By seeing clearly the ideal circumstances we need to have, we can now start to define the gap we need to bridge by acknowledging what we already have at the moment.

Ask yourself these questions:

1. By knowing what I ideally need to have, what are the things I *already* have right now?

2. What is in me that is a great asset?

3. What are the potential doors of opportunity that I have?

Knowing what your Purpose is and what you envision for the future is indeed a great asset. Not everyone your age has found their direction. Some haven't even found it at the age of sixty—which is okay, by the way.

Knowing what you're naturally good at is undoubtedly a treasure lots of people seek. Support from family or friends may feel like a normal thing, but it is like winning a lottery, or an award you once fought for. Take a look at your phone contacts, people in government, or relatives in the IT world, or old entrepreneur friends. What you currently have may not seem like huge capital, but *now* you understand how it can be a door to unexpected opportunities.

Current Assets ❯ Reality Gap ❯ Ideal Circumstances

Be clear about the current assets you already have. Don't forget to be grateful for them. You are one step closer to your ideal circumstances. Now you can realistically see the gap you want to bridge.

Your Current Circumstances

People have different conditions. Some are ready and have the capacity to go full time, others will need to temporarily take a part-time focus. This doesn't have any correlation with how courageous someone is. Instead, it is all about acknowledging the current reality and how to take smart actions. That includes making some adjustment while still being committed to pursuing the purposeful path.

While having total focus for pursuing a purposeful career path sounds ideal, it is also important to assess and map out the whole situation objectively. Be completely honest with yourself, and ask these questions:

1. *How do you see your current personal life? Do you have any inevitable responsibility to deliver that includes other people in the picture?*

2. *What should your main priorities be at the moment? Why is that so?*

3. *What would be the consequences if you neglected or delayed these priorities?*

4. *In your current circumstances, do you think you would be able to focus full-time on starting to live a purposeful career? Or, should you temporarily be a part-timer?*

Through understanding your practical conditions, you can see whether you are able to allocate full-time focus, or whether you should temporarily adopt a part-time mode. We will design the steps for your first lap according to this crucial decision.

Designing the First Lap

We know that living a purposeful career is not like climbing a mountain and achieving the peak. There will be multiple peaks and countless rock bottoms. The path will be long and endless. It will also be full of surprises. Therefore, what we will design together is not the whole journey of your purposeful career. We will zoom in on the very first lap you will take, once you have decided to start the marathon.

This first lap is crucial to setting the tone of the journey. Doing it in the right way will give you the right push and affirmation on the mission you are striving for. Letting Purpose drive you will form strong determination and spark the fun even in a challenging circumstance. Being ready to strive and manage perseverance will invite the unexpected door of opportunity to open before you. The duration of this first lap can vary, from one to three months, some processes can even take years.

In designing our first lap, first and foremost we need to be aware of the current reality gap we have. This is the gap between the ideal circumstances and the things we already have.

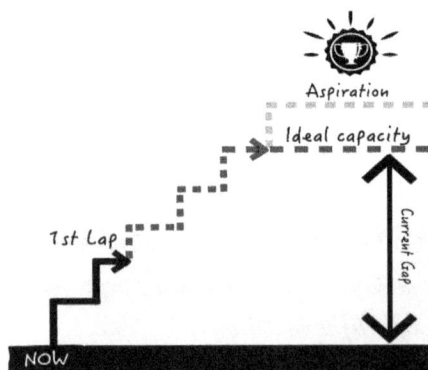

The first lap is constructed by the action you will take to get one step closer to the ideal circumstances. And, we will start taking a purposeful career path by exploring the LCD stage: *Learn, Connect, and Deliver.*

LEARN

As elaborated in the previous chapter, learning and development are always a combination of formal process, interaction, and experience.

> *Formal Learning – Interaction - Experience*
> *TO KNOW – TO UNDERSTAND – TO BE ABLE*

Doing extensive research prior to any practical experience can be useful in providing background and understanding conditions in the field. However, it is crucial to remember that effective learning will not only use your cognitive brain, but all of your senses, while being in that particular environment.

For instance, if you want to pursue a career in community development, the best way to learn and do your preparation is to experience the life of that particular community. Being in the exact environment and getting in touch with your potential customers, or experiencing the issues you want to contribute to, can be much more efficient than reading a book or doing research in a cubicle.

Estimated duration: 15 minutes

The following questions may help you to explore the areas you need to learn from in designing your first lap.

What to learn?

1. What are the knowledge and information you need to know in the career area you want to pursue?

2. Do you need to do further research in, and observations about, that area?

3. What are the skills you need to start learning and practice? What would be the basic skills that will bring you to the next level?

4. What can you do to sharpen the skills you already have?

Where to learn?

1. Where can you learn these skills? Do you need to take any specific program? Have you explored any online course that provides this particular program?

2. Would you consider financially investing in your learning, or do you want to start by self-learning?

3. Are there any specific places you need to go to expose your senses to real-life situations? Where are they?

Who to talk to?

1. Who do you need to talk to? Who are the key people who can share the information you need to know? Who are the people whose stories you are interested to learn from?

2. Can you think of someone who could possibly mentor you in this journey?

3. Do you need anyone to coach you, or help you practice your skills?

Based on your answers, can you identify or formulate **the three most feasible and crucial actions** in this area of learning you should do immediately? What are they?

1.

2.

3.

CONNECT

In the previous chapter, we explored the different circles of a supportive environment as one of the core tools of the warrior. We will now specifically focus on circle number 2. This is all about enabling a new connection, or maximizing the old ones. This could be the connection that will open the door and lead you to unexpected opportunities. It is the start of being in the right 'net' and, through conscious 'work', being connected with the right network.

Estimated duration: 15 minutes

Having seen the best network you need to have in the most ideal circumstances, we are now going to identify how you can get closer to that environment. The following questions will help you explore your necessary plan in designing the first lap, in the area of making connections.

Who to connect with?

1. Who are the type of people you see as being potential enablers in your career path? The type of people who could directly help and support you in executing your mission?

2. Who are the people or groups that could be collaborators in executing your plans? The people or groups who may have different missions but, connecting with them, will bring benefits to both parties?

3. Who are the people who could professionally support you in the pursuit of your career? These are people who might not work with you directly but, with their support, your process could be slightly easier. Through them you might connect with the right kind of people who could be your enablers and collaborators. These people could play a role as extended connectors.

4. Where can you find these people? Are there any specific places you could go to? Or, any communities you could be involved in?

How to connect?

1. Judging from your main character and personality characteristics (briefly re-read them on your first special page), what do you find most comfortable about connecting with people? What are your unique traits in forming human connection?

2. Are you confident with your networking skills? A networking event can be fun but it's definitely more than just exchanging business cards. It is also about effective listening and sharing stories, and building authentic connections. How can you sharpen your skills in networking?

3. How do you utilize your current connections to get in touch with a group of people you need to connect with?

4. How do you plan to maintain connection with your existing networks?

Based on your answers, can you identify or formulate the three most feasible and important actions in the area of connecting that you should perform immediately?

1. _____

2. _____

3. _____

DELIVER

Some may argue it is important to have a well thought out plan and a great deal of preparation before going into the field. Some say 'Don't go before you're completely ready'. However, in the dynamic world of the purposeful path, nothing is more crucial than to always validate your assumption. And the only way to do so is to start to deliver, as soon as possible.

Without a doubt, this is the one key action that can't be neglected. Starting to deliver, and having the opportunity to receive feedback, should be fully taken as the right and privilege of a purposeful fighter. And, this can be an easier case for those who are able to have full-time focus in the first lap. For others, if the condition is unfavorable, they must start right after they transition from part-time to full-time warrior.

Indeed, this stage can be like a double-edged sword. Getting one achievement could boost up your self-esteem in no time, while harsh feedback might make you face your worst fear. Therefore, as elaborated in the previous chapter, acknowledging your fear and choosing courage will be an endless battle. It is a choice to make before you start, and it is still a choice to make when you face bitterness. It is your conscious choice to learn the lesson then move on to be better and stronger, every single time.

There are lot of great things you can expect from delivering in the early stage. First and foremost, you get validation about what you think will be relevant and you get the most trusted feedback from your targeted market in order to develop your plan further. Secondly, you will see how it is the most effective way to sharpen your skills and tighten the learning process. Practice does make perfect. Delivering your prototypes or executing your pilot project is the best practice. In the area of motivation and determination, it is the best way to train your endurance. It is essential to taste the sweet, rapid successes and experience the small failures faster, so you can win better.

At this stage, you may want to consider whether to do the mission solo, have partners, or join another organization with an aligned mission. As was stated earlier, a purposeful career path should never be mistaken as a journey to entrepreneurship. Going for a purposeful career is not equal to starting a business. You can always adjust your decision later. You can even go back and forth. You can think of creating a prototype independently right now, then joining other people's projects later, or vice versa. Your circumstances may be different even a month from now, so keep your options open.

In a purposeful career path, you are allowed to have multiple ways to deliver your mission. Moreover, in order to keep on growing in different areas while being on track with your Purpose, there's no reason to create one rigid career plan. Flexibility for the right reason is gold! We call it 'purposeful flexibility'. It would be great, though, to decide what you want to do in the very first lap: whether you want to start delivering by yourself or with a team in an established organization.

Estimated duration: 15 minutes

Having seen the ideal activities you want to do in the most ideal circumstances, we will now identify the first steps to actively take on this first lap. These are the main objectives:

1. to validate assumptions, get feedback, and develop the ideas further

2. to get quick wins while minimizing the size of potential failures

3. to practically develop our skills faster

Our goal is to start delivering the values we have faith in as quickly as possible, in the simplest way, while learning and connecting. The following questions may help you in exploring the steps you want to take in starting your pilot project.

What to deliver?

1. What are the main assumptions you have at the moment that you would like to validate?

2. What are the essential values you want to contribute through your purposeful career? Ignoring all the marketing aspects you ideally want to create, what is the core essence of your product? Why do you believe it's what people need?

3. What are the current basic skills you have that you can utilize to start delivering that unique value?

4. What would be the simplest thing you can create, or start doing, to deliver that core essence? What would be your main channels in doing so?

Who to reach?

1. Who are the key people in the area, or situations, you want to serve who you would need to receive feedback from to validate your assumptions?

2. Think of the ideal target market you want to reach: their profile, their interest, age, educational background, even their gender and social status. Who are the people you know who would be the best representatives of your ideal target market? Who are the most fitting people to test out your product/service and give the most relevant feedback?

3. How many people would you like to reach in this first stage?

How to deliver?

1. Is there any other organization, or people, who currently do what you want to do? What are their similarities with your mission? Also, how are they different? Is it in the main market being targeted? Or, is it in the nature of the product?

2. Would you want to join an established organization to deliver the essential item? Or, do you want to create the prototype from scratch? Do you want to start experimenting alone, or is it crucial for you to start with a small team?

3. How would you prepare your prototypes, or pilot projects? What are the crucial aspects that need to be there in the process?

4. What is the best way for you to gather the feedback you need? How would you do that? How would you ensure your customer wants to share their honest feedback? Do you think a paying customer would give feedback differently compared to ones who got the product for free? Why do you think so?

5. How would you evolve and develop your plan further? Would you need to involve different parties?

When to deliver?

1. What is the shortest time for you to prepare the prototypes, or the pilot project? Remember: think of this as a way to validate your assumption in the simplest way possible. You don't need to make it perfect.

2. Would you need any specific timing to launch the product, or execute the pilot project? Why?

Based on your answers, can you identify or
formulate the three most feasible,
and important actions, in the area of delivery, that you should
undertake immediately?
What are they?

1. _____

2. _____

3. _____

So there you go, here is how the first lap in your endless

purposeful career path should look :

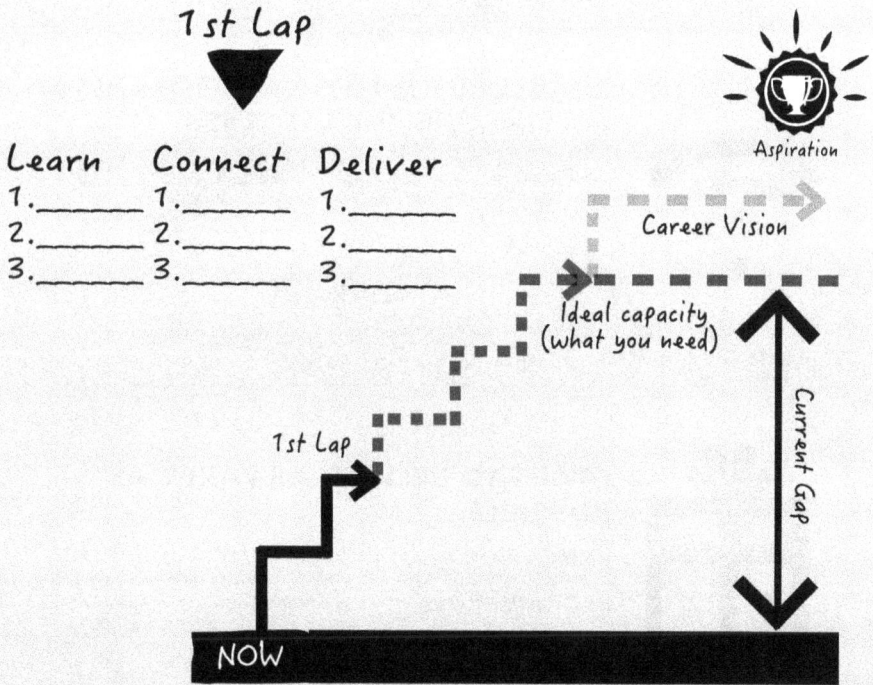

1 st Lap

Learn	Connect	Deliver
1.____	1.____	1.____
2.____	2.____	2.____
3.____	3.____	3.____

Aspiration

Career Vision

Ideal capacity
(what you need)

1st Lap

Current Gap

NOW

HOW TO DESIGN
YOUR 1ST LAP

A GREAT DEAL TO LEARN

Doing extensive research prior to any practical experience can be useful in giving background and understanding the condition in the field. However, it is crucial to remember that effective learning would not only using cognitive brain, but all of your senses by being in the particular environment. For instance, if you want to pursue a career in community development, the best way to learn and do your preparation is to experience the life in that particular community.

ENABLING THE NEW CONNECTION OR MAXIMIZING THE OLD ONES

Seeing from the ideal network you want to have in the most ideal circumstances, the process we need to do right now is to identify how we can get closer to that ideal environment. These following questions might help you in exploring your needed plan in designing your first lap, in the area of making connections.

START TO DELIVER AS EARLY AS POSSIBLE.

Delivering your prototypes or execute your pilot project is the best practical practice. While in the area of motivation and determination, it is the best way to train your endurance muscle. It is to taste the sweet quick wins and to experience small failures faster, so you can win better.

A Note for the Part-timer

For those of you who have decided to take a temporary part-time focus, the written output above might be a little overwhelming. Therefore, it is fine to not do everything at a sprint. The following sections will help you think about your concrete steps further.

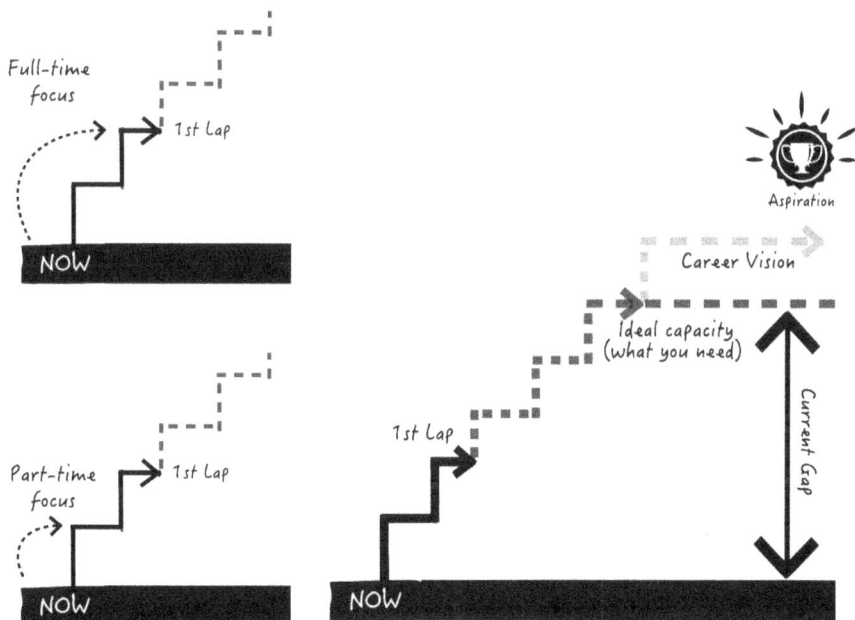

Full-time focus

1st Lap

NOW

Aspiration

Career Vision

Ideal capacity (what you need)

1st Lap

Part-time focus

1st Lap

NOW

NOW

Current Gap

The Other Thing

Your mind may be occupied with your urgent and important priorities. That's completely normal. Therefore, try to focus on how to meet these inevitable needs first. How would you meet your current urgent/important priorities? What is the wisest step to take? Someone who has some serious financial concerns, for example, might first need to take that full-time job with a decent salary to pay the bills.

One good option to think about is whether to take a job that will also give you a useful learning experience that aligns with your purposeful career plan. In that way, you'd automatically also cover your 'learn and connect' requirement. The next way to make a decision on this, is to be also aware of the company's vision and mission. Are they aligned with your personal values? Even if they don't directly contribute to *your* Purpose, would you be still happy to give your energy, time, and effort to help them realize *their* Purpose? Would you be excited, or would you be spiritually drained if you worked for them?

The commitment in that space around your clock

1. While performing your main responsibility, would you be able to allocate some time to start your own path? How many hours per day are you willing and committed to consciously allocate to doing the first lap of your purposeful path?

2. What would be 'the habit' you need to sacrifice in order to spare those hours in a day? Is it that two hours of watching a TV series? Is it that big chunk of hours scrolling your social media on lazy evenings? Or, is it checking updates on celebrities? Yes, friend, in order to commit, we *do* need to give up some pleasures.

Now, plan wisely and get ready to fight your future enemy

1. Looking at those action steps on your first lap plan, what are the top three action plans you need to start immediately?

2. How would you fit these top three into your available hours? If it helps, write the schedule down on your agenda, or block the specific times on your calendar, with reminders.

3. You know yourself best. What potential obstacles are there for you not to be committed to executing this plan?

4. How can you prevent these obstacles from happening? Or, how would you plan to overcome such a situation if it occurs?

5. What are the conditions you would need to support your process

and maintain your discipline? Do you need a coach? Do you need a learning group? Do you need constant reminders from your spouse or partner?

And, a really important note: questioning your Purpose along the way is not an impossible happening. Doing it full time is hard enough, doing it part-time needs an extra shot of stubbornness. There will come a time when you're too exhausted to juggle and will doubt your purposeful career plan. While doubting might be inevitable, the last thing you *ever* want to do is give up. Being different from the full-timer who is able to deliver and then gets validation and quick wins, you may have a delay in experiencing such pleasure. A part-timer needs a special tool for keeping their determination fresh and bold.

What would be the most effective reminder for you to sustain your motivation? To remind you of the relevance of your purposeful career? To remind you of the fulfilment you would gain from taking the worthwhile journey? What would work best for you? Would it be through reading books? Is it through traveling, once in a while, or participating in volunteer work? Is it through keeping a journal? Or, are you a person who can be reminded through having a powerful conversation with the right people? Who are the people you can count on? I know you must have names in your head.

One thing that is reliably useful is taking this method as a habit. Should you arrange a frequent conversation with that person? Do you need to read at least one relevant book every weekend? Explore your personality type, get to know what can work best for you, and be committed to the schedule that feeds your purposeful spirit.

The courageous jump

As mentioned earlier, sooner or later a full-time focus is a must to adopt. In order for you to be fully on track in your purposeful career path, there will come a time when you need to take that courageous jump: to make a transition from doing it part-time, to becoming a committed full-time warrior on the road less traveled.

Try to predict the signs or symptoms that will tell you when you are ready to transit to a full-time focus. Is it the moment when you are done with school? Is it when your mother is successfully finished with her medical treatment? Is it when your parents have moved to a better neighborhood? Or, is it when you reach a certain amount in your bank account? Be completely clear about the signs. Do not say something too general and vague like 'When I have enough money' or 'When I'm ready', because what happens if you just never feel that way enough?

If you need to, state your condition boldly to someone you trust the most. Write it down on your agenda or on that 'small piece of paper' and keep it in your wallet; you can get the sign when you are ready to courageously jump. This is your condition, this is your priority, and this is also your dream. You have every right in the world to go on your own path. And you *will* have the time.

Make Your Start a 'Star'

Hey, we are almost done with this dizzy puzzle! You may take a long deep breath now. I hope you are happy with your first lap design. I hope you are psyched up! I hope you can see that it is do-able. I hope you have faith that it is really possible.

I'll close this long chapter with some additional secret spices. From my observations of, and countless conversations with, purposeful career fighters, they do show some similarities. All of them admitted that the 'Start' stage is beyond thrilling! Sure, some parts were scary; but, they generally felt pumped up for finally taking that fateful first step. They felt an enormous positive energy. For some reason, the right opportunities just flew into their laps.

Some say it is 'beginner's luck'. That's a great term to define it because the continuous happy 'coincidence' won't last long. There are definitely more fitting opportunities along the way. The universe will support you when you do the right thing. But, regardless, the road will be rough. In facing the bumpy start, the purposeful fighters I know apparently shared some similar traits. They knew they would need way more than luck to keep going. They knew they needed some secret spices to make their start a 'star'. And, that is all based on attitude.

1. *Empathy*: *it means listening with your senses.*

   This is the attitude taken in choosing to genuinely listen and pay deep attention. It is not merely the case of listening to people. It is also listening to a situation and condition. Find the authentic Purpose you need to sense, to acknowledge, and understand how one thing happens, where it comes from, and how people feel about it. In most cases, empathy can tell you way more than you expect to know.

2. *Excitement to learn—endlessly.*

   This is *only* the very beginning of your journey. Rather than thinking you can harvest the impact tomorrow and smile gracefully for a better world, always have the excitement of learning. The first actions you take will reveal brand new information, lessons, and sensations. Always be excited for your personal growth during this process, and beyond it.

3. *Optimism.*

   Optimism is found in that area you will visit, those opportunities you will apply for, those people you will talk to, and in that decision to reject an offer that isn't right for you. In any first step you'll be taking, if you're like me, there might be a tiny voice inside your head whispering the question, 'Are you crazy?' Or, it could take the form of your friends asking, 'Are you sure you want to buy that one-way ticket? Are you crazy?'

   The first step you take can be really, *really,* far from your comfort zone. It might seem very challenging, but when you know your clear reason and you have the path you have carefully designed, *take it*. Be bold, for it is gold. It is challenging, but believe me, it can be beyond rewarding.

4. *Adaptability*

Yes, the first step is gold, but it might not go according to plan. Most likely, it will go quite far away from the original plan. A couple of purposeful fighters who do battle in the agriculture sector once shared with me. Their bank accounts were completely washed up just months after they started their project. They needed to adapt to the situation and find a way to make it work. They now stand stronger than ever, years after having zero in their savings. Expect that you will meet some failure, and then get ready to restart in a better way.

5. *General positivity*

Have joy. That is one of the keys to opening the doors of limitless opportunities. I have nothing more to say.

This has indeed been a pretty long chapter, with tons of questions, that didn't seem like it would ever come to an end. It was a long process that required honesty, and your authenticity, in designing a single path that is yours, and yours only.

Seeing the distant vision has been exciting, but frightening at the same time. When we have the humility to be grounded, we are able to lay down our majestic dream in small concrete steps. When we have these little concrete plans, we're taking one firm step: one firm step at a time in this long, endless, exciting ladder of a purposeful career.

Chapter 11

Connecting the Dots

It has been quite a journey. It has definitely been one for me and I hope, as well, for you. Writing this final chapter, I can't help but wonder how you will be feeling after all we've been through: what's in your mind and in your guts after the process throughout this book.

You might put this book down on a messy table, currently full of written papers, sticky-notes, markers, or any other tools you've been using during your personal 'me-time' with the book. You might have tidied up your journals and taken this book to bed and read it in solitude to close the day. You might have wanted to finish this book as soon as possible, and directly start your journey.

You feel excited, your heartbeats and your guts are telling you so, with a pinch of fear and doubt in your heart. At this very second there are thousands of people in different parts of the world—whether they're reading this book, or another book, writing journals, or having a meaningful conversation—who feel exactly how you're feeling. It is your heart, and their hearts, that are sending signals to listen to your personal calling and start the adventure.

I have told you since the beginning that this book project is something very personal for me, and I hope it has become personal for you as well. This book is driven strongly by one belief: if human beings could live a career that is aligned with the reason for their existence—to make a living out of something they love doing, that they're good at, and to give positive results to their surroundings—it could create a continual snowballing effect. I have no doubt that the world would then be slightly better.

For some reason, I get the feeling you will resonate with my belief when you take your adventure. Though it might sound like putting our heads in the clouds to watch unicorns and rainbows, we know for sure that the process will not be simple. It all starts by understanding ourselves, finding our true self, and listening to ourselves in the middle of this noisy world.

Looking back to the earlier journey, we understand that listening to ourselves attentively can bring us to something bigger than ourselves: it can bring us to understanding the role we play in life. We got to explore Purpose: something we had heard about somewhere before, that had been roaming about in our heads for quite some time, or that was just introduced and we were unsure if it was actually within us.

Purpose takes form within moments in our lives when we know that our life isn't just passing by like the wind. Our lives have meaning and reason. At the end of the day, a career is a thing that occupies a huge portion of our lives. Developing and living a career with Purpose as its essence is like riding the right vehicle on the right path in the right direction: it will bring us closer to a sense of fulfillment, while improving the state of the world we live in.

From the first time the idea of this book came to me, you have always been the core inspiration. This whole book is about facilitating your journey in discovering, designing, and living *your* purposeful career. It is all about assisting the story of your endless rollercoaster ride to come. It is about getting to know, and being in touch with, the three big elements that form your Purpose and exist within you.

This book explores Passion, that gives joy to your soul; Talent, the inborn gift; and Contribution, that gives meaning. It has been a process of discovery enabling you to go on some adventures. You have taken different kinds of adventures: in your own mind, in your drawings, in your handwriting, in your conversations with people you trust, and in some new places. These adventures might have gotten you lost, only in order for you to find yourself again: to find your Purpose.

Purpose is found in the intersection of these three elements, when you can finally discover what role you can play within your lifetime. Since a purposeful career is what can bring you closer to the realization of Purpose, envisioning your career journey is one crucial step toward designing the direction of your path.

Making a living out of something you love, and you're good at, while contributing positively to society, is a journey worth living that requires clarity of destination. Not that this is any guarantee we can achieve that during the journey, but it works as an aspiration to keep us moving forward on the right track.

We always know that the whole journey will be challenging and dynamic. The journey to fulfillment is far from easy. It is endless but worthwhile. It is certainly less traveled. Before making a turn and starting a journey, a great deal of preparation and equipping oneself in the right way is always needed for an adventurer—for a warrior. All the tools have been placed in your backpack: the tools to choose courage, to build your skills, and to gain the right support system.

We've almost reached the finish line of this journey of ours, which will also mark the beginning of your *own* fulfilling journey. It doesn't mean you'll be all by yourself in going the distance. This will sometimes feel like a long, winding, lonely road but, believe me, you are not alone. You never will be. You are taking the purposeful journey together with other adventurers on different roads. You might meet each other along the way—for a short time, for a momentary lesson, or it could be for the rest of your life. You might also meet me again, when it is time for us to take another journey together.

Let Me Leave You With...

I will leave you with one final story about the lessons I got from learning how to ride a bicycle at the age of twenty-five.

Until last year, I was incapable of driving anything for, in my whole life, I had always depended on public transportation to commute. Yes, I couldn't even ride a bicycle for some reason that would need another whole chapter to explain. When I decided to move to Bali in 2015, I eventually needed to force myself to drive. I started the process of learning through riding a bicycle. I didn't realize at the time that, through this process, I learned so much more than just how to cycle.

It only takes a couple of days for kids to learn to ride a bicycle when they are five or seven years old, but it took a couple of weeks for me. The main reason is the older you are, the higher the level of fear you have. A two-year-old won't stop learning how to walk when they fall down. A five-year-old will cry for five minutes when they fall from a bike, but then they will wear their bruises proudly.

The first few days of my lesson, I was too cautious because I didn't want to fall at all. I was afraid of the pain. I had enough experiences in life to know how bruises and scratches are uncomfortable, thus I tried my best to avoid them. But, the fear of failure puts us at risk of not choosing the opportunities worth taking. So, in any case, it's better to start the journey to do your purposeful career as early as possible.

I'm not saying you need to invest all your savings into one project and pray to have it magically work. I'm saying: pick up that pen and paper; make those phone calls; go to the area you've always been curious to observe; write the very first page of the book you're longing to write. Because, when you take that leap of faith, there's nothing you will lose, but your fear.

After being able to ride a bicycle in a park, going onto a big road is a different game. It felt scary at the time, but the objective of my learning to cycle was not only to ride in a safe area. To develop yourself you need to have the courage to put yourself outside your comfort zone; to eventually stretch the zone, so it is much wider. Have strangers evaluate your work and give you feedback. Put the sample of your product into the market, take to the public stage and talk.

Once you go into the wild, into the real world, your senses will help you to not crash and enable you to adapt. This will help you get through those challenges in the unknown. However, no one says you can do it with just zero preparation. At least I knew how to turn and use the brakes before going onto a big road full of cars and motorbikes, so I knew how to protect myself.

Riding a bicycle looks easy, but it was very difficult for my adult muscles to pick up the skill of how to move my legs properly and synchronize my brain with my body. It needed ongoing practice and process—everything does. Nothing is instant—except instant food—yet when we look at other people succeeding in work on their project, it seems easy.

When we hear it 'took 10 years to become who they are right now', we think of ten years as one long line of a journey. We seldom think that it is pretty much 3,650 days—87,600 hours full of practices, storms, bruises, trials and errors—to become who they are at the present. And, they are not done yet. They continue practicing and trying different things to keep improving their skills, no matter how awesome they are in our eyes. The more you know things, the more you will realize there is more to explore in this world. That's why geniuses are humble and always eager to learn.

On the first few days of my bicycle lessons, I approached them the way I attended math classes in high school. It was intense and full of pressure—literally. I applied too much pressure every time I moved one of my legs, which obviously did not help in keeping my balance. Only then did I realize, in order to keep my balance I first needed to be calm and relax while keeping my legs moving.

The journey of a purposeful path is endless and can be stressful, but you should still enjoy it in balance. Your soul will give you signals when you do too much. Listen to it. Those people who are called to realize their Purpose will be able to do their best when they are in their best shape. Health, relationships, and other elements in your being, play just as important a role as Passion, Talent, and Contribution in the quest. When you realize that you have put too much pressure on one side of the bike, you need to make extra effort to go back to the right position. Then you can keep on moving.

So in summary, here are the life lessons I got from learning to ride a bicycle at the age of twenty-five:

- Start early! Take that leap of faith, you have nothing to lose but fear itself.

- Prepare yourself to venture out of your comfort zone, then widen your comfort zone.

- Nothing is instant: you have to learn more, practice more, and do more, to get better.

- Be in balance and enjoy it.

Realizing what our Purpose in life is can be seen both as a burden and a gift. I would like to see it as a blessed mission. Our life is short, yet we spend so much time during our productive age in working. Though it's not the only source, our career contributes a huge portion to our happiness. It is definitely not a coincidence that we find happiness in doing positive actions for others.

Having a purposeful career is a long endless journey—it is not a destination. Celebrate every milestone while remaining persistent in taking one step forward at a time. It is indeed a blessing. Our Creator wants us to enjoy the process and be grateful for having the courage in taking the right path.

Life is short. In such a short period of time, every human being must have a role in leaving a mark—no matter how big or small—to enable the world to evolve positively. I'm doing mine, and I hope you listen to *your* calling.

Enjoyed your journey with Turn Right?

Please consider posting a short review. Honest reader reviews help others decide to start their adventures with the book.

May you always have the courage to live purposefully!

Acknowledgements

At any intersection, a human needs to make a decision: to take the turn, to go straight, to go back, or to stand still. The journey of writing a book about purposeful careers started from a lucid dream, and was followed by one decision to take a sharp, fixed turn. A hope for a possibility always welcomes inevitable fear as sweet company. I'm forever grateful for having the following people, who helped me choose to see the bright light over the shadow of fear—over and over again.

To Puri Lestari (the writing partner I met at one unexpected intersection and who decided to walk with me on the long journey of the incubation and delivery process) a huge appreciation for choosing to stay and push forward, and—most importantly—for believing.

Having Theodora Wiroreno by our side as editor has been beyond my wildest imagination as a newcomer in the self-publishing world. Thea has assisted the development and evolution of Turn Right, from one first messy page to the next fifty thousand-plus words. She's just always there—literally, always.

Our illustrator, Dacik Juwita, has enriched the soul of Turn Right through her authentic and vibrant drawings. A number of people with big hearts—Michelle Anindya, Max Rempillo, Brett Merril, Adityah Kasim, and especially Michael Linden—came at the right time and have given the significant final nudge for the birth of this book. I can't thank them enough!

And a high five to Hans Baetsen, for being a hand to hold, not only in the final sprint of the book, but also in this adventure called Life. Looking forward to a thousand cups of hot chocolate, and more!

There are some brilliant minds and warm hearts that have been my source of energy along the way. For the continual massive support and learning, my deepest sincere gratitude to: Fiona Ekaristi, Jihee

Jeon, Andri Agassi, Andina Dwi Kanti and Dea Rezkhita (the fearless girls in Bali), Soraya Rosadha and Dayinta Pratiwi, Arief Ambiya, Victor 'The Great Moustachio' Lesniewski, Elisabeth Hannia, Sandro Rayhansyah, Jenn Hadi, Apresty Renjani, Sri Annisa, Olga Melinda, and Blandina Pella. I also really appreciate the insightful conversations I had with Ali Zaenal, Edwin Djakaria, Astuti Martosudirdjo, and Ayleen Wisudha, which have provided some inspirations in the development process of Turn Right. There is a special place in my heart for some great friends I met in AIESEC, the International Congress CC Team, the supportive people at Kumpul Coworking Space and Outpost Coworking space, Global Shapers Denpasar Hub, the Dream Catchers from IOMW, and a number of beautiful souls from FISIP Unpar 07.

And a very special couple of names I'd love to mention: Yohannes Lie and Kumalawati. In the middle of any life confusion, there are three magic words every child always wants to hear from their parents: 'I trust you'. We may see and experience life differently, but they are the first ones who taught me the real meaning of compassion and struggle. They let me continually explore, take risks, learn, and strive for a greater good. They believe in me. This book would never have even been started without their unconditional faith. This book is dedicated to them.

Finally, to all the dreamers who are scared but still take the leap anyway, to you who read this book, thank you. Thank you for listening to your authentic self. Thank you for taking that sharp, fixed turn. Enjoy the ride!

Bibliography

Gallup, Inc. "What is the difference between a talent and a strength?" Accessed November 16, 2016. http://strengths.gallup.com/help/general/125543/difference-talent-strength.aspx

Google. "Google's mission is to organize the world's information and make it universally accessible and useful." Accessed November 16, 2016. https://www.google.com/about/company/

Green, Christopher D. "A Theory of Human Motivation by A.H. Maslow (1943)." In Classics in the History of Psychology. Originally published in Psychological Review, 50(4), 370-396. Accessed November 16, 2016. http://psychclassics.yorku.ca/Maslow/motivation.htm.

Koltko-Rivera, Mark E. "Rediscovering the Later Version of Maslow's Hierarchy of Needs: Self-Transcendence and Opportunities for Theory, Research, and Unification." Review of General Psychology Vol.10, No 4 (2006): 302-317. Accessed November 16, 2016. American Psychological Association. DOI: 10.1037/1089-2680.10.4.302. adapted with permission.

Luks, Allan. "Helper's high: Volunteering makes people feel good, physically and emotionally." Psychology Today 22(10), October, 1988. adapted with permission.

Shontell, Alyson. "80% Hate Their Jobs -- But Should You Choose A Passion Or A Paycheck?" Business Insider, October 4, 2010. http://www.businessinsider.com/what-do-you-do-when-you-hate-your-job-2010-10.

Sorensen, Kathie and Steve Crabtree. "Exactly What Is Talent, Anyway?" Business Journal – Gallup, October 2, 2000. http://www.gallup.com/businessjournal/412/exactly-what-talent-any-way.aspx

The Economist. "Mission statement." Accessed November 16, 2016. http://www.economist.com/node/13766375

About The Author

Inez Natalia is a facilitator, author, traveler and lifelong learner. She is passionate in supporting people to explore, design, and live their purposeful career. For thousands of young people in over fifteen countries, she has facilitated group workshops, conferences, team experiences, and one-on-one consultations in the area of self-discovery, leadership development, team building, and career planning. She's a big enthusiast of the coworking movement, where she observes and participates in the evolution of various purposeful careers in today's world. She currently resides in Bali, where you can find her riding her white bicycle on the beach or sipping her morning (and afternoon) coffee.

About The Intersection Project

The Intersection Project is the brainchild of Inez Natalia and Puri Lestari. It's a place for young people to gather and contemplate their strengths to have the right focus to achieve a purposeful life. We believe in a purposeful life and career. We are dreamers, doers, and contributors. We believe that if together we live our lives purposefully, the world will become a better place. Don't we all crave this? Get connected!

theintersectionproject.com
hello@theintersectionproject.com
fb.com/theintersectionproject

www.ingramcontent.com/pod-product-compliance
Lightning Source LLC
Chambersburg PA
CBHW051724040426
42447CB00008B/960